# TUSCAN HARVEST

*By the same author*

\*

CALF LOVE
TOPSY TURVY
UNKNOWN SOLDIER
THIS IS MY LIFE
TOMORROW ALWAYS COMES
GO EAST, OLD MAN
STRUGGLE FOR AFRICA
REPORT FROM MALAYA
AND NOW, TOMORROW
TUSCAN RETREAT
A BOOK ABOUT ELBA
INTRODUCTION TO ITALY
THE PAST OF PASTIMES
THE COLOUR OF THEIR SKIN

# Tuscan Harvest

VERNON BARTLETT

*With illustrations by*
MAURICE BARTLETT

1971
CHATTO & WINDUS
LONDON

Published by
Chatto and Windus Ltd
40 William IV Street
London, WC2

\*

Clarke, Irwin & Co. Ltd
Toronto

ISBN 0 7011 1659 5

© Vernon Bartlett 1971

Printed in Great Britain
by Ebenezer Baylis and Son Ltd
The Trinity Press, Worcester, and London

M

*This book is for Jo, the
Lady of the Postscript*

# *Contents*

| CHAPTER | PAGE |
|---|---|
| One | 11 |
| Two | 52 |
| Three | 98 |
| Four | 130 |
| Five | 170 |

# Chapter One

THIS book is, to some extent, a sequel to *Tuscan Retreat*, published in 1964, of which a reviewer in *The Spectator* wrote that it was 'a pleasant book, but a distinctly middle-brow one'. That hurt me a little; 'middle-brow' was so clearly a derogatory word. But I had to admit that, although I have been called many things, nobody, as far as I know, has ever called me a 'highbrow' or an 'egg-head'. And I found comfort in the thought that there are far more 'middle-brows' than 'high-brows' in the world, so there must be far more people who might be interested in the only kind of book I can write than there would be if my brow were of unusual height. Nevertheless, you have been warned.

Why do I write it? Why, above all, a sequel? For a variety of reasons, of which one is that many people have asked at different times about Giuseppe, Berto, and Gino, who work or have worked on my little farm, and who are men of such simple wisdom that I enjoy writing about them—at this very moment Giuseppe and Gino are out with the truck, shovelling great mounds of cow manure on to my largest field, and the beauty of these dark mounds, *couleur tête de nègre*, on the *café au lait* shade of the sun-dried soil, with the red truck in the foreground and a background of the tree-covered Pisan Hills would persuade any artist to set up his little easel and to get out his paints, or any writer to pick up his pen. Gino and Giuseppe are creating a beautiful picture, even though they don't know it.

Other reasons for this book? It will make a little money but, believe it or not, that is by no means the most important consideration (principally, I admit, because the sum thus earned is not likely to be large enough to make much difference to my life). Much more important is the chance it gives me to get in a word edgeways, and I enjoy putting my thoughts down on paper, even if not many people read them. I am now an old man, and Somerset Maugham—of all people!—wrote that one of the major compensations of old age was that 'it liberates you from envy, hatred and malice'. It was scarcely true in his case; if it happens to be nearly true in mine, then this book will have some small value in a world where those unpleasant qualities find such frequent expression. One needs to get away from them, and if this is escapism, it is escapism with good purpose. 'Why bother about the future?' asked Mark Twain. 'Has the future ever bothered about us?' But to bother about the future is one of the strongest of human or animal instincts—think of all the efforts made by parents to leave their children better prepared to face the future than they were themselves. I have not yet reached the stage when I shall cease to worry myself (and other people) about the way we run the world ('we' when it's running well: 'they' when it's not).

Indeed, my reluctance to fade out of the picture, to realize that the world could get on just as well without my advice—indeed, it could hardly fail to do so; my advice, in broadcasts, books and articles, has been about international affairs, and look at the mess they are in!—very nearly brought me back to live in London after the publication of *Tuscan Retreat*. The book had been published a few days after my seventieth birthday, and had received a welcome which revived ambitions I had thought were dead—I had deliberately condemned them to death ten years previously, when I had left England to start life anew in South East Asia. My publishers had launched the book at a flattering cocktail party. The reviews had been exhilarating. Sidney Bernstein had collected a dozen of my oldest friends at a dinner. Other old friends had welcomed me back. There had been the Garrick Club, with the silver reflected by the polished mahogany and the Zoffanys hanging in the dining-room (still mysteriously called the 'coffee room' in clubland) and the talk about books and politics, wine and pictures (the ones that hang on walls, as well as those on cinema screens). I had been immensely stimulated by this attractive and civilized atmosphere, and the regrettable fact that more people are not in the fortunate position to enjoy it was not to my mind a reason for wanting to abolish it altogether. This was my kind of London and I loved it. I 'belonged' again.

And, above all, television had gone to my head. In the days of 'steam radio' I had first faced the microphone at 2LO, Savoy Hill—a microphone the size of a television set which blew all its valves if one raised one's voice—in 1924, and had begun, in January 1928, a series of weekly talks that had lasted for six years. I had immensely enjoyed those meetings with the microphone (although my diary for January 25th, 1928, records: 'Gave the first of my "Way of the World" broadcasts. Very depressed about it; think it was bad. Violently sick in the night'). I spent many hours improving a technique designed to convince the listener that I was thinking aloud, with, at the most, a few notes in front of me. I was therefore terrified of the world of television, in which I could not have before me a script with emphatic words underlined, significant pauses marked, and with minutes and half-minutes noted in the margin to make sure that I did not commit that worst of all B.B.C. crimes—overrun my time. 'Steam radio' had done no more than carry my disembodied voice through the loudspeaker to families whose members might be doing the washing-up or waiting impatiently for the dance music that was to follow my talk. TV, on the other hand, would confront these families with my face, and the thought gave me no pleasure and was unlikely to give pleasure to them.

But on the occasion of this visit to London, I overcame my distrust of television, and I found that my three short appearances on the screen had been enough to cause several people whom I did not know from Adam or Eve to pause, and to wonder whether they knew me. 'Who's that chap?' I could almost hear them thinking. 'I've seen him somewhere. Oh yes, I know; he was on the telly, talking some tripe about something. I've got it! He was talking about his little farm, somewhere in Italy. Lucky devil! Sitting on his backside all day in the sun!' I had so enjoyed broadcasting; for a few foolish minutes, I thought I might have the opportunity to make regular appearances on the television screen.

In the case of the regular commentator, whose face appears on the screen evening after evening, the effects of such recognitions must be, quite literally, appalling. No more for him the blessed anonymity that can be one of the greatest attractions (as also one of the saddest features) of life in a large city. No chance, outside his own home, to relax. Is my tie straight? Dare I look as tired or as bored as I feel? Shall I be caught out if I pick my nose? One wonders that so few of them suffer from nervous breakdowns. But for a fellow like myself, brought out of obscurity once in a while to take part in some television programme, this ephemeral fame can be very stimulating.

I found it so. For the time being, I forgot my age. I forgot that I had inevitably become a bore, at least to younger people, who were now the very great majority. I forgot that the enthusiasm shown by my friends would fade when the surprise of seeing me round the place had worn off. I forgot that it would be ridiculous, at the age of seventy, to resume the social and political ambitions that I had so deliberately renounced at the age of sixty. I was very sad to leave London.

It was stickily hot when we arrived at Pisa. I had given the wrong date for our return, so there was nobody to meet us. My tour of the *podere*, the little farm, was disappointing— weeds outnumbered the oats in our fields; there would be very few peaches and the birds had already taken almost all the cherries; there was no promise of flowers on the olive trees that, the previous season, had given us half a ton of olive oil, and I refused to be comforted by Giuseppe's reminder that as a rule olive trees produce a good crop only in alternate years. The vines looked healthy, but my short experience of farming in Italy had already taught me that many disasters could happen to the grapes between the early summer and the *vendemmia*, early in October.

During our absence two years earlier, Giuseppe had run up a formidable bill for water in order that everything should be fresh and green on our return; this time, he had not dared to use the hose, and the lawn, the making of which had been my special task and pride, was already brown, except where the tougher brands of weed had taken over and had smothered the more delicate grass seed, imported from England. (I am often distressed by the formality of Italian gardens, which are planned as part of the architecture of the villa they surround, for I hate to see trees lopped and pruned into all sorts of artificial shapes; I was surprised when an Italian friend told me how he hated to see a formal English lawn, devoid of all the daisies, dandelions and other flowers that would so readily grow there.) And Annunziata, who will tend the vegetables with the greatest care, sees no value in flowers, so that the drought had killed most of the roses. Since my facial expressions show my feelings much more clearly than they ought to do, my wife, with her customary patience and resignation, was convinced that we should be trying to sell the *podere* within a year.

Within a day or two, I recovered my balance. If I were living in London, a long connection with the B.B.C. and the over-mobile face referred to in the preceding paragraph might possibly have brought me a good deal of television work. So what? Inevitably, in a few years, I should find that ambition had gone too far ahead of diminishing achievement. I might earn much more money than I now have, but I should certainly have far more things on which to spend it. Above all, I should lose my peace of mind.

Not that I find much of it even here in Italy. Within a few hours of my return from London, the reaper came to

# TUSCAN HARVEST

cut our wheat. Our fields are long and narrow, on terraces built across the hillside. Along the top and bottom edges of each terrace, separated by a ditch, is a row of vines. The large and clumsy reaping machine has inadequate room in which to turn, and the constant reversing gear that this inadequacy makes necessary is bad for the mechanic's temper and my vines. Given the nature of the terrain, it is difficult to devise a better system, but it is bad both for my pocket and for my peace of mind.

No European farmers I have watched at work are more industrious than the Italians, with their small hill farms, but the odds are against them. Even if they had the capital with which to buy the finest agricultural machinery—and in this respect they can get reasonable loans from the government—they could not hope to compete successfully with the large-scale farmers of the plains. One day I showed Gino, our *contadino*, a photograph in an American paper of the latest combine harvester. He looked at it without curiosity or envy; it was almost as remote from his world as the various contraptions now circling in outer space are remote from mine.

The reaping of our wheat coincided—as it often does in Italy—with our hay-making. Each afternoon, black thunder clouds emphasised the difficulties that beset the small farmer. In those days we had to take our turn to hire the plough, the reaper and the threshing machine. We therefore could not do the work when the clouds most clearly indicated that it should be done, for there was a long list of farmers waiting to hire the machines. On this particular occasion we were lucky—the two stacks, one of oats and one of wheat, were built and the hay was safely in the barn before the weather broke, and rain blessedly drenched the vines, so that the grapes seemed to double in size in less than a week.

But such luck is rare. It may be that the farmers in Britain are doing well—I hope they are, for they need some good luck to compensate them for the tricks played on them by the weather. I hope, for their sake, that my small-holding provides more problems than does a large and properly organized farm. The man whom I have most admired as an agriculturalist was the late Laurence Easterbrook, and he once wrote to tell me about farming in England that 'you have to farm a thousand acres pretty badly to fail to make £2,000 a year by exploiting it, but you have to farm well to make a living off a hundred and fifty acres'.

What hope, then, have I, with my fifteen acres? My chances of success are so small that I take great care not to work out what is our production per acre. Even if I kept the strictest accounts, I should not really know how much I was out of pocket at the end of each year, for Giuseppe is not paid principally to work on the farm, and I cannot estimate how much more I should have to spend if we had to buy our eggs, our poultry, our milk, our maize, our vegetables, our fruit. And if I had no land at all, I should probably spend money in other ways. I might even lie awake at night wondering why I had sliced that drive at the seventh tee or why I had had that extra drink at the club. I might find no better way of passing the time than to walk as far as the local café and home again.

And although my *podere* does not leave me with the anticipated peace of mind, at least my worries do not bring me into jealous competition with my fellow-men. There remains, of course, the problem of winning and retaining their respect. In my case they are Gino and Giuseppe, neither of whom has ever left the land for a week except when Mussolini's war suddenly dumped one in Jugoslavia and one in Greece. And nothing wins their respect except success in the cooperation or competition with the seasons. At least in one aspect of that subject they consult me with deference—they expect me to tell them what the morrow's weather will be. They have virtually no conception of the points of the compass—to Gino, an east wind becomes intelligible only as a wind from Pistoia, and the south-west wind, that brings us our rain, must be defined as a wind from Pisa. So, even if he listened to the weather forecasts on the radio, he would not be much wiser. I have the advantage over him in that respect. Also, I tap a strange, clock-like instrument that is a barometer. Above all, I have had long experience of the English climate.

The climate of Italy is normally so steady—except during the thundery period in summer—that Italians have never learnt, as most Englishmen have done, to study the morning and evening sky, the height at which the swallows are flying, the behaviour of insects and flowers, and, most of all, the twinges of rheumatism or the agonies of gout (which I prefer to blame on the climate and on my ancestors than on those two or three extra glasses of my wine).

My paternal grandfather was a most lovable country

parson, clean-shaven except for a fringe of white hair that stretched under his chin from ear to ear, as though he were wearing an Elizabethan ruff. A gentle old man, and it may be unfair to attribute to him my tendency to gout, for he had ten children to educate, and certainly could not have afforded to spend much on alcohol. Nevertheless, he, too, suffered from gout, and one of my very early recollections is of this godly man in his armchair, with one foot wrapped up in masses of cotton wool and propped up on a stool. Between his legs was his cello; he was sawing away at it in the hope of forgetting the pain. And I, a clumsy little boy, knocked against his bandaged foot.

I have no recollection of the word he used. Probably 'dash'; possibly 'damn'; just conceivably one of the grosser and more explicit four-letter words without which no book is now up-to-date. I cannot even recollect how I knew that the word was not one to be used in polite society. But my shocked surprise that it should be used by so gentle and holy a man has survived during nearly seventy fairly crowded years.

But the *podere* calls for so much more than some understanding of the weather. When should we cut the corn? When should we spray the fruit trees and the vines? What spray should we use for the potatoes? Which shoots should we prune on the olives? How long should we leave the grape juice to ferment in the vat? Should we add tartaric acid? When should the wine be racked or fined? I leave to Giuseppe as many of these decisions as I can, and each time I thus try to conceal my own ignorance, I am back in my imagination on the barrack square near Weymouth early in 1915. In common with thousands of other youths who have suddenly been commissioned, I am trying to avoid a crisis by saying: 'Carry on, Sergeant!' and my two Italians are just as tactful as my sergeant used to be in helping me to retain some semblance of dignity.

\* \* \*

Gino and Giuseppe? Here must come a few pages of explanation, even at the risk of boring readers of *Tuscan Retreat*, who may still remember Giuseppe and the circumstances that brought him into our lives. They won't know Gino, for neither did I when I wrote that book. For a variety of reasons, the most important of which was a motor smash which put my wife for many weeks in Lucca hospital, we bought a villa five miles outside that ancient and attractive city. A villa, in Italy, is not a small, semi-detached affair in a suburban road; it is likely to be a very large house, with out-buildings and several acres of land. Ours is a small villa, but, nevertheless, a much larger house than we needed, so that in the attic there is a room as large as a London flat, with one window facing up the hill, over the tops of the olives, to the church of San Ginese, and another window facing over the valley to the Pisan Hills, covered with pine forest and rising to a height of three thousand feet. A beautiful room which, however, is used only for suitcases and unwanted pots and pans. At least the villa is not so large that we have to leave a dozen rooms or so to ghosts and spiders, as is the case with so many Italian country houses.

Apart from the view, two features persuaded me to buy the villa. One was the wine *cantina*, containing six large barrels, one of which can hold nearly eight hundred gallons of wine. (It has not done so in my time; the other, smaller casks suit us better for too many of the vines died off in the years of neglect before we bought the place.) The second feature was the stone table at the side of the house, where we could have our meals under a pergola which is covered in spring by wistaria, in summer by the red and orange flowers of bignonia, and in autumn by virginia creeper.

When I paid the money over to the grubby old farmer who had owned the villa, I had barely considered the agricultural aspects of the deal. Indeed, I had not even walked round the frontiers of our land. My failure to do so must have amazed the vendor; to him, as to any other farmer, the land mattered so much more than the house that was built on it. Or, to be more accurate, the houses, for, in addition to my own large, square house, there is an attractive, long, low building, one part of which is a home for the farm-labourer and the other part is for the cows on the ground floor and for their hay in the loft above them. I knew that there were rather more than two hundred olive trees, some thousands of vines, a dozen very small fields, and three small copses. But I did not know that these few acres would occupy so much of my attention, and that Giuseppe and Gino would become so important in my life.

Giuseppe and his wife, Annunziata, were there from the start, and we chose them mainly because one of her brothers was a policeman; it seemed prudent to be thus associated with authority. Giuseppe, as an old farm labourer, I told myself, would know what to do with the garden and the farm, but I did not at first realize that I should never be able to carry on a discussion with him, since he speaks so indistinctly that even his fellow-Pisans find it hard to understand him. He has learnt his language entirely by sound, without recognizing the individual words. (The only letter I have received from him was to announce that they were busy mowing the hay—'*siamo a tagliare il fieno.*' But this he rendered as '*sia amo attagliare il fieno*'.) This phonetic rendering would make conversation difficult even if he had not so strong a Pisan accent and if he were less in the habit of using the wrong words ('*Consorzio*', for example, becomes '*concorso*', which is something very different). Even his Lucchesian neighbours often find him hard to understand, and at times I am compelled to humiliate him by appealing to Annunziata to interpret—this hurts him, for he treats his wife with as much condescension as would be shown by any Moslem. When he goes out with her to cut food for the rabbits, she carries home the heavy bundle and he carries the scythe. Had I anticipated the misunderstandings that would arise from this barrier of language, I should not have engaged

Giuseppe, and thereby I should have lost one of my most valued companions.

His monosyllables are his most intelligible forms of speech —indeed, the meanings that most Italians can get into an 'ah', an 'oh' or an 'eh' is remarkable. In the middle of a discussion with Annunziata, Giuseppe will suddenly say 'eh', and that is the end of the discussion; there's no more to be said. If I call out for Annunziata, her reply is 'oh'. The ejaculations are short and sharp, and they require a much more open sound than can normally be achieved by the English who, more than any other people except the Danes, swallow their words and talk through almost closed lips. The meanings of these ejaculations also depend on intonation; they are part of a tonal language; they can be affirmative, incredulous, interrogatory or, especially with Giuseppe, downright challenging.

Through friends, we engaged Berto, who was to be our full-time farmer. He arrived with his stout, jolly wife and his extremely elegant little daughter, Antonietta. He was so conscientious as to be rather slow, and this earned the contempt of Giuseppe, impulsive and rather slapdash (and constitutionally incapable of bolting a door both top and bottom to prevent it from warping). The feud between Pisa and Lucca has gone on for many centuries, and I have already described in *Tuscan Retreat* how much it embittered the relations between these two men. It even robbed Giuseppe of his normal kindness when Berto fell out of an olive tree he was pruning, and seriously damaged his back. Never could one forget that Giuseppe was a *Pisano* and Berto was a *Lucchese*.

For a little more than a year after his accident, Berto stayed on in our *contadino*'s cottage, so ashamed because he could do no heavy work that he seldom sat outside in the sun, while Nunzia, his wife, tried to earn his wage as well as her own. The strain was too great. It was mainly to escape from farm work that Giuseppe had come to us in the first place, and here he was back on the farm, doing the old chores on behalf of a man whom he disliked. He became almost morose. Nunzia became less and less jolly—although she still sang when she was working in the fields, since she had been told that song was useful to keep away snakes— and more and more worried by the shocking difficulty of getting Berto his disability pension. The olives had no trenches dug around them, to be filled with manure or with woollen rags to hold the moisture; the earth under the vines was left unturned; the acacias—those damned, sweet-scented, sharp-thorned acacias—advanced more and more boldly from the copse into the olive orchard. The ditches were filled with weeds—the surest indication of a neglected farm. My wife was increasingly distressed by the difficulties of keeping the garden in order without Giuseppe's help, and I was more and more distressed by the many fruitless interviews on Berto's behalf with members of parliament, mayors, councillors and other officials. Even if we found Berto some job, how should we find another *contadino* to occupy his cottage and to look after the *podere*?

But, when the prospects seemed as black as could be, Gino turned up. Annunziata mentioned one day that her brother-in-law wanted a change from his present farm, the owner of which had just died. She thought Gino and her sister, Maria, might like to come to us. An interview was arranged.

I was, at first, appalled. I had never met anybody like Gino. He was one of those fat Italians whose belt does not encircle his stomach, but goes beneath it to give it support. His face was very round and very, very red. He talked almost incessantly. But what alarmed me during that first interview was the way in which he strutted round, his hands in his pockets and his stomach stuck out aggressively. He might be, as Giuseppe assured me he was, a good worker, but he would almost certainly be even more difficult than Giuseppe himself to keep under some kind of control. With my insufficient knowledge of Italian, my difficulty in understanding their dialects, and my ignorance of farming, Gino and Giuseppe would become my masters, not my employees. I should have the privilege of paying them a lot of money to order me about.

But what agreeable masters! What willing workers! We found Berto a light job in the village where he was born, and where he is now happy, with no Pisan about the place to despise him and order him around. Gino, I discovered, had put on an act at that first interview in order to conceal his own shyness. He had to remain in his previous job until the harvest had been brought in, but he was determined to help us. During the months that elapsed between Berto's departure and Gino's arrival, Giuseppe milked our cows and did other essential jobs, but Gino managed to come over twice or three times a week, bicyling seven miles each way but arriving nevertheless shortly after six in the morning, and not leaving again until after seven in the evening—with, admittedly, time off for his siesta.

And, once Berto had left, with his belongings piled high on a lorry, and Giuseppe had therefore become convinced that I, a sentimental Englishman, had not decided to keep an incapacitated man permanently on my staff, there was a dramatic change. Giuseppe's reluctance to do work on the farm was replaced by his determination to do it. He and Gino became inseparable. In temperatures rising to over thirty degrees Centigrade, they dug along the rows of vines, one on either side and neither more than a yard ahead of the other. While pruning the olives, they kept close enough to each other to carry on their interminable conversations from tree to tree. Together they set out, with heavy tanks strapped to their backs, to spray the vines (and themselves) turquoise-blue with copper sulphate. Side by side they scythed the *passi* that would give the reaping machine access to our small fields of oats or wheat. In winter, each wore a beret clapped to the side of his head; in summer, each wore a coloured straw hat of the kind Italy now exports to seaside resorts all over the world or caps with large peaks, such as are favoured by American tourists wearing Hawaii shirts, but bearing lettering to advertise (in Giuseppe's case) a brand of vermouth and, in Gino's, a brand of fertilizer. Occasionally, Gino would appear in a kind of bishop's mitre, fashioned out of an old copy of *The Times*; on such occasions, with his jovial red face, he would have been an admirable model for one of those dreadful nineteenth-century paintings of a lot of monks sousing wine at a long refectory table. Except when the wind was in the wrong direction, I could generally tell in which part of our fifteen acres the two Gs were at work by the sound of their laughter or their songs.

Gino has a very Italian voice—the kind of voice for which his fellow-Lucchese, Giacomo Puccini wrote his operas. Giuseppe, on the other hand, has the high-pitched and (to northern ears) almost tuneless voice that one associates with the Arabs. A voice that might well belong to a muezzin chanting verses of the Koran from the mosque. A voice that reminds one how strong the Moslem influence once was throughout the Mediterranean area. Giuseppe's ancestors, being Pisans, were probably dragged into wars against the Saracens, the Turks, the Barbary pirates, whose activities led to the construction along Italy's coasts of fortresses or watch towers to give warning or shelter to the peasants and the fishermen when the hated sails of these Moslem slave-raiders appeared over the horizon. The crescent and the cross have both ceased to be used as emblems to justify piracy or conquest, but, among evidences of former Moslem power are the spotlessly white villages of southern Spain and the strange, melancholy music of Mediterranean Europe. Turning the knob on my radio in the hope of hearing the B.B.C. without atmospherics, I pick up music from Algiers, from Tunis, from Cairo and so on, and, for all the difference that I can detect, it might come from Andalusia, from southern Italy or from Giuseppe in my own vineyard.

Berto had been excessively ready to take off his beret and to address me as *Signor Padrone*. This I disliked, but not, perhaps, as much as I pretended to—I am not by nature a leader, but it is rather nice to be treated as one. Gino went to the other extreme. If I said something that amused him, he was likely to thump me heartily on the back. This, too, I rather disliked, but his actions were so spontaneous that nobody could really be offended by them.

For four years my two closest associates and friends have been these two shabby and untidy men, Giuseppe and Gino, each wearing at least one garment that I had discarded because it was so patched. Then—less than twenty years ago —every afternoon on five days a week, I walked down the Duke of York Steps with a brief case, a rolled umbrella, a black hat and nicely polished shoes, indistinguishable from all the civil servants returning from their clubs in Pall Mall or St James's Street to their gloomy offices in Whitehall. I was not, in fact, one of them, but I would be on my way to the Foreign Office, and had taken on the same protective colouring. I belonged to the Establishment; now, thank God, I belong to the village of San Ginese.

Here, in parenthesis, two paragraphs about shoes. When I lived in Rome in 1921 and 1922, I could not sit for two minutes outside a café without being importuned by a shoe-black; brilliant shoes were as much a status symbol in Italy as a rolled umbrella in London. Nowadays, the shoe-shine boys have entirely disappeared, and Italian men go around in shoes that are still elegant, but are often aggressively dirty. And, paradoxically, this change is evidence of greater prosperity—there are so many more jobs than there used to be, bringing with them so much more money that it is no longer worth anybody's while to kneel between the café tables, shining other people's shoes.

The second paragraph has nothing to do with Tuscany. In 1920, when I was correspondent of *The Times* in Switzerland, I was invited to lunch to meet Count Berchtold who,

as Foreign Minister in the Austro-Hungarian Empire in 1914, had been primarily responsible for the declaration of war against Serbia and, thereby, for the world war that followed it. I expected to find an old man, bowed down by the memory of his appalling responsibility—or, rather, irresponsibility. Instead, I found a dapper and complacent man whose one memorable comment during the luncheon was to the effect that I was very lucky to be an Englishman. Why? Because only in England did they know how to clean brown shoes.

Gino wore no shoes at all in hot weather, despite the pieces of broken bottles and the rusty tins that one finds about the place—after our arrival, we moved eleven sackloads of such garbage from under the elegant box hedge. The disposal problem is a difficult one, for there is no system of rubbish collection in our area, and we have no alternative but to keep a box of empty tins and other such stuff in the boot of the car, to be emptied at some spot—often the bank of an other-wise charming little stream—where everyone else is dumping rubbish. But some tins and bottles did not get even as far as the boot of the car—they remained about the *podere*, a menace to the shoeless Gino.

When, shortly after his arrival, we stacked our wheat in the lower fields to await the arrival of the threshing machine on its long tour through the neighbourhood, he took over from Giuseppe the position of authority on the top of the rick, with the responsibility of packing the sheaves, sloping up-wards and pointing towards the centre in such a way as to reduce the ill-effects of thunderstorms or hungry sparrows. The rick grew higher and higher, so that the sheaves could no longer be lifted to him on our hay-forks, but had to be passed up to Giuseppe on the truck, and by Giuseppe to Gino on the summit of his hill of grain and straw. When at last the job was done, Giuseppe proposed to fetch the ladder, but Gino waved the suggestion aside. This wasn't necessary; he could slide down the side of the rick to the ground.

While he was still in mid-air, I noticed that he wore no shoes, and that he was coming down on the short, sharp stubble that I found uncomfortable even when I had thick-soled shoes. Hadn't he hurt himself, I asked anxiously. Stuff like stubble, he boasted, meant nothing to him. Why, some years ago he really had cut his foot, and had done it so badly that they took him to the hospital, where the doctor told him he would need six stitches to sew him up. But after the fourth stitch the doctor gave up the struggle; he could not force the needle through the leather that Gino had grown on the soles of his feet.

A few hours later, I saw Gino and Giuseppe going off, each with his spraying tank on his back, to the old, over-

grown vineyard on the west slope. There are plenty of snakes
in that part of the *podere*, since my neighbour's land on that
side has not been cultivated for years. Although most of the
snakes are harmless, turned into innocent enemies by human
fear and prejudice, I had seen a small one which looked to
me like a viper, so I followed Gino down the slope to warn
him. He searched in the pocket of my old pyjama jacket
which had somehow become the garment in which he went
spraying, and produced a jagged piece of glass. 'This stuck
into my foot a little while ago,' he explained, as though it
were the greatest joke in the world, 'and it didn't hurt. No
snake is likely to do so.' Away he went down the row of
vines, boastful, bumptious, ludicrous, and yet somehow
dignified and lovable.

\* \* \*

Gino and Giuseppe must remember those ricks with as
much displeasure as I do. The former, strongly supported by
the latter—or it may have been the other way round; they
are so alike that one is apt to get them confused—argued that
we could save ourselves and the threshing team a lot of
trouble if we built our ricks in the lower field instead of in
the courtyard of the villa. Indeed, the drive up to the villa
is so narrow, and the branches of the alternating limes and
ilexes so impede the passage of anything wider or higher than
an ordinary car, that the threshers had declared the previous
year they would never tackle it again. We must build our
ricks, they said, in the small field at the bottom of the drive.
This would be convenient for them, since their machine
could remain on the road; it would be very inconvenient for
us, since there is no proper access to this small field for the
cart that would carry our sheaves. But one dare not argue
with the owners of the local threshing machine.

I reminded Giuseppe and Gino of all this. But the previous year, they pointed out, none of us had realized that
there was quite a reasonable road leading out of the bottom

field, in which, very conveniently, our oats were stooked. This road passed through a *podere* belonging to an old lady known as Emma—a ragged old lady with very bright eyes and a fantastically patrician profile—and she was willing for us to use it if she might build her own rick on our land. The road was not paved, but it was fairly level, and the threshing machine should be able to negotiate it without difficulty. I continued to raise objections, mainly because I had not thought of this solution myself, but I was easily talked over. So we built our ricks in the bottom field, where their relative insignificance was cancelled by Emma's own much smaller one.

This we did early in July, when the threshing machine was still miles away at Porcari—at one time, the home of that formidable eleventh-century ruler, the Countess Matilda of Tuscany (from whom, I believe, comes the name Tessa or Tess). The machine was not due to reach us until the very end of its long tour of duty. For over a month, every morning when I looked out of my window, those ricks caused me a little stab of worry. They were not thatched, although Gino had spread a layer of hay on the top of them. Every day, the menace of a thunderstorm darkened the sky, and brought the shade temperature nearly into the nineties; would not one real storm stimulate the ricks to sprout untimely green shoots, or cause spontaneous combustion that would burn the heart out of them? I was immensely relieved when Giuseppe told me one morning that Guido, the owner of the threshing machine, wanted to see me.

'We can't work in your lower field,' he announced. 'The road's impossible.'

I bundled him into my car, and drove him along it. There were more formidable bumps than I had expected, but I emphasised that a surface which nearly threw us out of a small Fiat would not matter to a machine that weighed eight tons. When we reached the field itself, he used my argument against me; the ground might seem rock-hard to the driver of a small Fiat, but it would not prove rock-hard beneath a machine that weighed eight tons. His *trebbiatrice* would shake itself into deep grooves from which it might be impossible to extricate it; we must transfer our ricks to the field at the bottom of the drive, and we must do it within twenty-four hours, as the *trebbiatrice* was at the end of its tour, and he wanted to pay the team off.

I pointed to Emma's small rick. She had an invalid husband, and nobody to help her. How was she to get her oats moved and restacked at such short notice? Guido responded, as almost all Italians do, to this appeal to his sentiments. There were almost tears in his voice when he referred to her, but he dared not risk the mishaps to his *trebbiatrice* which would be involved if he followed our road. Gino and Giuseppe still believe that he would have yielded had I been more persistent or more subtle—had I hinted, for example, that he lacked courage—but my unfortunate temperament enabled me so to share Guido's anxiety that I ended up almost by congratulating him on his decision to inconvenience us.

Emma wept when we broke the news to her, and was exaggeratedly grateful when I said we would move her sheaves as well as our own—an easy decision for me to reach, since Gino and Giuseppe, and not I, would have to do the extra work. I had previously told them of my intention to help Emma in this way, and they greeted it almost with sulkiness. At any rate, with a lack of enthusiasm most unusual for them. But as soon as they saw Emma in tears their attitude was completely reversed; they worked until the hottest hour of the day to rebuild her rick on its new site. By doing so, they strengthened one of my conclusions about the Italians.

There is, in Italy, a most dangerous lack of civic sense, which leads to contempt (emphasized, rather than concealed, by too much cringing flattery) towards people in authority, and also to a very frequent tendency on the part of people in authority to make use of their power to line their pockets with public money. Here is one small example of this lack of civic sense. Recently, in Lucca, an unattended bicycle toppled over, and the contents of a basket attached to the handle-bar poured out on to the road. At first, nobody moved to help. Then one woman joined me in collecting the stuff and putting it back in its basket. I felt both conspicuous and indignant. Had the bicycle's owner been present, probably everyone around would have cooperated in picking up the scattered vegetables and small parcels but on this occasion the human hyphen was lacking; it occurred to nobody that the mishap to the owner was just as great in her absence as it would have been had she been there. Once, figuratively speaking, Emma stood weeping in front of her rick, Gino and Giuseppe were generous in their help to her. And she, after thanking us with a dignity which would have done credit to the Countess Matilda herself, helped in the threshing with an agility which filled me, her contemporary, with shame that I could not emulate her.

The process of threshing must, at the best of times, be so noisy and dusty that it almost cancels the satisfaction of seeing the grain pouring into the sacks. (And how few sensations are as satisfying as that of plunging one's hand deep into a sack or bin of wheat!) On this occasion, the whole process was beastly. When the *trebbiatrice* arrived, the only piece of our land on which it could expel the chaff was the self-same small field on which stood the ricks and, as ill-luck would have it, there was a stiff breeze which blew it straight back at us. Emma, Annunziata and Maria, Gino's wife, stood on the ricks to feed the sheaves to the conveyor belt, and, with the chaff blowing past them, they were at times as indistinct as if they were involved in a heavy snowstorm. With Gino tackling the heavy bales of straw at one end of the machine and Giuseppe filling the sacks with grain at the other end, there was not much for me to do except occasionally to help their wives in this storm of chaff.

I had already been humiliated during the building of the ricks in the first place. While passing up the sheaves to Gino, I must have handled my hay-fork clumsily, and I wrenched a muscle in my left hand so badly that I had to keep my arm in a sling for nearly a week. During the threshing, Annunziata, Emma and Maria were compelled to work directly to windward of the scudding chaff, and yet

they escaped with nothing worse than a rather comical untidiness; I, far less involved, got straw dust so firmly lodged in my eyes that I could do no work for a week and had to go to the doctor for treatment. My efforts to take part in running the *podere* are all too often both painful and ridiculous; on such occasions, I go around rather ostentatiously with books and sheets of typescript to remind the two G.s that there's one subject about which I know more than they do.

\* \* \*

The cynical Italian attitude towards their politicians and the frequency with which financial or other scandals show some justification for the cynicism go far to explain why one meets so many people who argue that life under the Fascists was not, after all, too bad. At least, they say, one knew where one stood. It was, of course, very annoying to be ordered about by all these strutting Blackshirts, but discipline imposed from above may, at times, be less annoying than self-discipline—as schoolboys soon learn when they are put on their honour to behave well. And peculation under a dictatorship may be less hypocritical than peculation wrapped round with fine phrases about democracy, liberty and the sovereign will of the people.

Many of the Italians who infuriate me by talking in this way about Fascism have, of course, no recollection of the real thing. I have, for I was one of those who watched the lorry-loads of young and yelling Blackshirts hurtling down the Via del Tritone on that morning of October 28th, 1922, and, with Edgar Mowrer of the *Chicago Daily News*, I had the first interview with Mussolini when—the 'March on Rome' having been successfully carried out by his Fascists—he arrived from Milan by the night train. And I remember, as younger people cannot remember, that Fascism was a reaction not against Communism, as Mussolini liked to argue, but against a whole series of weak and inefficient governments, put into power by the exercise of universal suffrage.

I loathed Fascism and I loathe it now, as I loathe Communism or any other 'ism' which sets out to diminish the value of the individual. I am as convinced as ever I was that any system of government imposed from above is more degrading, although in all probability temporarily more efficient, than any system that grows up from the grass roots.

But, despite this undiminished hatred for Fascism, I am less ready to condemn than I was some forty-five years ago. I know decent Italians who would now vote Fascist if they had the chance to do so. I know decent Spaniards who still believe they were right to support Franco during the civil war. I know decent Frenchmen who hold that they were justified during the war in following Pétain rather than de Gaulle. The older I grow, the more I am compelled to admit that views I detest may be held by others with a sincerity equal to that with which I hold mine.

Who can be certain, for example, that the Frenchmen who escaped from France, often at very great peril, were in every case purer patriots than other Frenchmen who decided that they must stay in their country to support Pétain, in the belief that he was still seeking to alleviate the hardships of his compatriots and to keep alive the sentiment of 'Frenchness'? I know that, at the time when the invasion of Britain seemed inevitable, I went around with an uncomfortable little bag of money tied round my middle, since I had decided that in no circumstances would I leave my country. Had Hitler successfully invaded Britain, should I, somewhere in hiding there, have later been condemned as unpatriotic by those of my compatriots who had got away and were training somewhere in North America for the liberation of Great Britain?

I came across a rather similar problem in a milder form in Singapore shortly after the war. Heaven knows there was reason enough at that time for the Europeans to forget any little differences between them, for the Japanese had done everything they could to destroy the myth that the white man is born to rule over other men. The Asians had seen their white masters of yesterday marching off, in rags far worse than their own, to break stones at the roadside or to empty latrines, under blows or kicks from their new Asian masters. And yet, after it was all over, one found the Europeans of Singapore nearly as divided as the Gaullists were divided from the Pétainists.

Smith, I would be told, was quite a decent fellow, but he was one of those who had run away. He might subsequently have served his country far more effectively than he could possibly have done had he stayed and had been locked up in Sime Road or Changi jail. But the fact remained that he had escaped from the burning city in some ship, and when the war was over some of his compatriots were sure to suggest, ever so obliquely, that he had 'ratted'. Then there were the other arguments. Jones, I would be told, was quite a decent fellow, but he had been one of those who lacked the guts and the initiative to get out in time. He might have suffered terribly at the hands of the Japanese, but some of his compatriots were sure to suggest that he spent an unnecessarily long time swaggering around in his prison rags after the liberation of Singapore. Brown, I would be told, was quite a decent fellow, but his truculent behaviour in the internment camp had led the Japanese to inflict dreadful punishment on all his fellow-prisoners. Robinson, I would be told, was quite a decent fellow, but his efforts to obtain some improvement in internment camp conditions looked to some of his compatriots very like sycophantic collaboration (only much more vulgar words would be used) with the Japs.

I doubt whether, when we pass judgement on our neighbours in matters of conscience, we pay enough attention to the temptation to follow the line of least resistance. It is so much easier to conform than to contradict and the motive for doing so is not always cowardice. It is so much easier to be indignant about *apartheid* in a country where all but two or three per cent of the population is white than if one belongs to a white minority surrounded by a black majority. It is so much easier to uphold the rights of man in a country where there is no danger that the dawn knock on the door will be made by two policemen with revolvers and jack boots. It is so much easier to become a member of the Party if all your neighbours are also becoming members of the Party.

There is, of course, something else besides this geographical or social influence on one's conduct, and besides the metabolism that makes one man gloomy and another man cheerful, one man an introvert and another man an extrovert, one man a socialist, worrying about the good life that may be created in the future, and another man a conservative, worrying about retaining what is good from the past. There is what is generally called one's conscience, something so intimate and so personal that I doubt whether any outsider has the right to interfere with it. The conscientious objector has a shamefully difficult time of it during a war, since anyone who refuses to act as most of his neighbours are acting must inevitably become the object of suspicion and dislike. And yet, even in this case, with its concomitant dangers to the security of the state, most civilized governments do now recognize the importance of the individual conscience.

This being so, I, as an individual, find myself less and less anxious to judge and to condemn. God knows I hope the Italians will not return to dictatorship—selfishly, I reflect that, were they to do so, I should have once again to start house-hunting, and in another country. But, were they to do so, my feelings towards them, at the moment of their acceptance of dictatorship, would be less of indignation and reproach than of sympathy and pity.

Indignation, it seems to me, should be expressed at a much earlier stage, when the ordinary individual needs no special courage and very little effort in order to behave as a decent citizen. People who leave litter about the place, who form gossiping groups on busy sidewalks, who stand on the wrong side of the escalator, who try to jump the queue—these people deserve more blame for dictatorship than does the harassed father of a family who joins the Party (whatever the Party's political complexion) because he may otherwise lose his job.

And in this respect I admit that Italy fills me with disquiet. In Britain, somebody once said, everything that is not specifically forbidden is allowed; in Germany, everything that is not specifically allowed is forbidden; in Italy, everything that is forbidden is allowed. So much more is forbidden than seems either wise or necessary, so many outdated laws that were passed in one or other of the many small states of which Italy was composed before unity was achieved in 1870 are still on the statute book, that the result is confusion. And in Italy, more than in any other country I know, ignorance of the law is disallowed as an excuse.

Vernon Jarratt, an English friend who owns one of the most famous restaurants in Rome, gives a list, in his *Spaghetti in my Hair,** of the thirteen documents an Italian has to produce (or had to produce until very recently) if he wants to have a passport. He also tells a splendid story of a man who found himself called upon to pay a tax on his horse although he had never possessed such an animal. He consulted a lawyer, who explained that in one way or another, his appeal against the tax would probably cost rather more than the tax itself, even without taking into account the cost of the lawyer's advice. So, after sending in a protest on *carta bollata*, the stamped paper one has to buy for some shillings at the nearest tobacconist's in order to lodge an official complaint, he decided that he would, in this one instance, pay the tax. But his official complaint was mislaid in the government department to which it had been sent, and the next year along came a fresh demand. This time, his protests were met with incredulity—how could he pretend he had never had a horse when, last year, he had paid a tax for one? Once again, after consulting his lawyer, he decided it would be cheaper to pay up, but on the third occasion he was ready when the tax demand arrived. The horse? Oh, the horse was dead. And he took some tax official out to his back yard to see the very dead remains of a horse which he had obtained, at considerable expense, from a near-by knacker's yard. That, he thought, would put an end to all this nonsense.

Not a bit of it. The authorities, the tax official explained, would need a declaration—on *carta bollata*, of course—from a veterinary surgeon to confirm that the horse was dead,

* Leslie Frewin, London 1965.

and was, in fact, the animal on which the tax had been paid for the last two years. Then there would be the matter of an abattoir licence, since the animal had obviously been killed. And the Sanitary Office would have something to say about decaying organic matter near a dwelling house . . . The mythical victim of taxation muddles ended up with a term of imprisonment for assault on an official engaged in the execution of his lawful duties.

In my own case, I recently received a demand for payment of a special tax levied on 'luxury' villas. But, except in the matter of bathrooms, this house falls short of almost every one of the several conditions which, under the law, amount to luxury. Nevertheless, I had to engage a surveyor in order to obtain a six months' postponement of payment while the authorities made investigations. Since this surveyor had once worked in this particular department, he was on 'old boy' terms with its present occupants, and doubtless this led, after I had made two quite considerable payments, to the admission that the original demand had been a mistake. Could it be possible that the official and the ex-official had developed a small but profitable racket, based on tax demands that should never have been sent? Yes, it could, although I do not believe it in this particular case. And could it be possible that I am incurably naive? Yes, it could.

I have a further tax worry. Because I am an Englishman, accustomed to the receipt of a stern warning from British Income Tax offices when my payments are due, I cannot remember, in the absence of any warning, to pay my various Italian taxes. The result is that I do nothing about them until I receive a notice informing me that I am '*moroso*', which means not that I am morose, but that I am in arrears with my payments, and am being fined in consequence.

I am, of course, aware that contempt for the law, with destructive and sadistic undertones, is now, more than at any other time for at least a century, an alarming fact all over the so-called civilized world. But much of this contempt seems to arise from the difficulty of adapting oneself to relative affluence—it is, perhaps, strongest in the wealthiest countries. This affluence, for example, gives rise to the problem of how to use unwonted leisure, and it is much harder to find a solution in a cold, wet climate than in one where the sun makes *dolce far niente* so very agreeable. So it may be that, in the long run, the senseless and beastly attacks of callous cruelty and vandalism in Britain will be more damaging than the Italian chronic tolerance of lawlessness. But those of us who lived in Italy during the two years preceding Mussolini's march on Rome cannot help noting the similarities between the situation at that time and the situation today.

One needs to remember that Italy became a united nation only in 1870—the much more publicized union of 1860, brought about by Garibaldi, Mazzini and Cavour, who are commemorated by statues or street names in every Italian city, left out Rome and what remained of the Papal States. In immediately preceding centuries, the Italians had been governed by Spaniards, Frenchmen, Austrians, to say nothing of scores of princelings serving the Popes, the Emperors of the Holy Roman Empire or, above all, themselves. Under foreign rule, breaches of the law become acts of patriotism. A plethora of princes, kept in power by force and intrigue, encourages the sycophants and discourages an honest and efficient bureaucracy. Promotion depends less upon ability than upon a *spinta*, a helping word put in on one's behalf by a powerful man at the right moment. This dependence, indeed, was one of the most noticeable features of the Roman Empire, where most of a citizen's morning was spent either in encouraging his own 'clients' to boast about his power and generosity or in flattering the man higher up the ladder on whom his own progress depended.

One could hardly expect such a background to stimulate the development of a sturdy democracy. Recently, at a parking place in Lucca that was officially full, I asked the attendant whether I should be safe to leave my car for half an hour outside the white lines painted on the ground. He shrugged his shoulders and gave me a typical reply. 'Who can say? Every policeman makes his own laws.' This, I decided, was so true that I thought it worth while to send a picture postcard from Cape Town to the policeman who normally controls the parking times on one of Lucca's principal squares, and as a result of this mild form of bribery, he now interprets the law in my favour. On the other hand, several of the very narrow streets in the very centre of the town have at last been closed to all wheeled traffic, but even respectable citizens—to my puritanical fury—often fail to dismount from their bicycles in these streets.

The hotel industry, of such importance to Italy, since the tourist industry brings more than twenty million foreign visitors each year to the country, is governed by a law of 1937, which laid down that an hotel was in the first category if it had a well-furnished lounge with a radio set and at least one bathroom on every floor. But it is also governed by a law passed in 1925, according to which each hotel occupant must have thirty cubic metres of air space, whereas only eighteen cubic metres have to be provided in new apartment houses. So, if the law were carried out—which it, of course, will not be—a large number of newly-erected hotels would have to be pulled down again.

In June 1965, *Time Magazine* claimed that twenty-one different application forms had to be filled up before electricity could be supplied to a Rome flat. It took the author of the article four months and seventy-one telephone calls to get number plates for his car. (I suspect that the procedure would have been much shorter had he gone round to the ministry involved and chatted up one or two of the officials concerned.) 'More than 250,000 veterans of World War Two and their families,' the article went on, 'are still waiting to start collecting their pensions. At the present rate, their applications will not all be approved until 1987, since, as one study shows, it takes fifteen days for the *"burosauri"* [the bureaucratic dinosaurs] to send a letter from one floor to another of a ministry. As late as 1954, the government was still reimbursing Sicilians for damage done to their ancestors' property during Garibaldi's historic campaign to unify Italy.' The article ended by remarking that the Department for the Reform of the Public Administrations had had fourteen heads in seventeen years.

I quote this article at some length partly to console people elsewhere who are cramped and cribbed by the growth of their bureaucracy, but mainly to show how dangerously the patience of the Italians is being strained. My newspaper today contains these evidences of unrest: 'Barricades and tumults in Turin during a strike against high rents' states the banner headline across the front page. This page also prints details of a conflict inside the Socialist Party over the attitude to be adopted towards the very powerful Communist Party. Paragraphs on other pages deal with a strike of local government employees; a strike of clerks of assurance companies; strikes in local cotton and jute factories; a refusal by the Association of Industrialists of the Province of Lucca to receive a trade union deputation of more than five persons because, on the previous occasion, some thirty delegates invaded the building and broke several of the windows; an attempt by law court employees to break into the Ministry of Justice; and the announcement that a two-day strike of postal employees is to be replaced by a 'go slow' week, which will revert to a national strike if, at the end of the week, no solution is in sight. On the last occasion of this kind literally millions of letters and parcels were held up, and letters from England took nearly a month in transit. Last week, most of the trains were held up by a strike of station-masters. At a time when many people are demanding that British police should be armed, to deal with a people that is normally notoriously law-abiding, the Italian Communists are campaigning for the disarming of the Italian police, who have always been armed, and riots at Battipaglia, in Southern Italy, and elsewhere have convinced the police that they will not have full government backing in the event of very serious trouble.

*    *    *

Possibly an experience some years ago has unfairly deepened my pessimism. Our villa is administratively in the parish of San Ginese but geographically in that of San Leonardo (in that the road to San Leonardo is less steep and considerably shorter). So we find ourselves called upon to contribute money to the festivals organized by both churches. Although I go to neither, I do not greatly resent this double imposition, for these festivals provide the only organized amusement the

farm workers around me ever get. As far as I know, Berto and Nunzia, Giuseppe and Annunziata, Gino and Maria, did not once go to a cinema or to any kind of entertainment except a family wedding, a birthday, or a festival to commemorate some religious event in an entire year.

These church festivals are much alike. The village is decorated with little flags, flowers and coloured electric lamps. In the evening, the statue of the saint is carried through the streets or lanes, preceded by a band, generally very damaging to Italy's reputation as a musical country, and followed by scores of adults and children carrying lighted candles. Neither of our parishes is important enough to attract even one merry-go-round, but the main street is lined with stalls for the sale of plastic toys, sacred images, or sticky sweets. And, of course, there are fireworks—no Italian festival is complete without rockets, just as no Chinese festival is complete without fire-crackers.

Once every three years, for example, at the neighbouring village of Massa Macinaia, there is a celebration in honour of *La Madonna della Cintola*—the Madonna of the girdle—on so splendid a scale that hundreds of sightseers come to it. They watch the long procession of flickering candles winding over the hill. They crowd into or around the church. They wait impatiently until the bell-ringers spring into sudden activity to announce that the church service is over and the time has come for the fireworks. On a recent occasion, all these fireworks were given by an American—an Italo-American, of course—who had been born in the village and who had travelled from the States in order to be present on this important day. His fireworks, the noisiest possible rockets, were the finest I have ever seen. The evening was a great success.

A few weeks later came the turn of San Ginese, whose church crowns the hill on the southern slope of which stands our villa. San Ginese cannot compete with Massa Macinaia in the matter of wealthy emigrants, but there were plenty of people taking the short cut through our *podere*—the evening of the San Ginese festival is the only time during the year when we think of copying the normal Italian procedure, and of closing the gates of the villa since, on our very first year, some local merry-maker stole all my seven lemons. There was a buzz of conversation from St Ginese's one street, all along the crest of the hill, loud enough to rival the buzz of conversation in the Strand on a warm Sunday evening.

After one visit to this festival, we have preferred to watch the fireworks from an attic window. I know there will be no Catherine Wheels or other set pieces, such as used to make the display on the evening of the Bournemouth Regatta so memorable when I was a boy; I know in advance that no display can be as exciting for me as were those relatively humble efforts of Messrs. Paine and Brock, the two great firework manufacturers of my boyhood, as seen from our favourite spot on the West Cliff. But I have to admit that their rockets were mere squibs compared with the splendidly noisy and colourful rockets with which Italians commemorate their saints.

So, on this particular occasion, my wife and I went to the attic window as soon as the first rocket exploded into its many-coloured stars. There were three more of them, and then a long pause. There was a bright pink glow from the region of the launching pad—or do rockets still soar from the neck of a bottle, as they did in the days before V–1s and V–2s? This year, we told each other, San Ginese had surpassed itself; there must be some fine set-piece of which we could see no more than the reflection. But we waited impatiently for the next rocket.

There was no other. Within at most a couple of minutes the pink glow was replaced by high flames. After five or six weeks of drought and heat, some sparks from one of the rockets had set fire to the neighbouring woods. There was a strong breeze, and great clouds of smoke, shot with sparks, hid from us the crest of the hill. They recalled to me the most awe-inspiring sight of my life—the view from Fleet Street up Ludgate Hill to St Paul's, on that December night in 1941, when the Germans tried to burn London into submission.

A large fire was burning somewhere near Blackfriars Bridge, and for most of the time the smoke from it entirely concealed the cathedral. But occasionally the cloud of smoke and sparks blew away for a few seconds, to reveal the great dome, with the golden ball and cross glowing with the reflection of the flames from another huge fire, in Cheapside. And, as though nothing untoward were happening, black and dirty trucks were being shunted to and fro across the bridge that spans the bottom of Ludgate Hill. The view was both terrible and inexpressibly beautiful.

Our fire at San Ginese was in a different category. It was frightening, but not awe-inspiring, spectacular, but not magnificent. The wind was blowing from the north-east, and not in our direction, but within ten minutes or so, the flames had spread so far down the hill that they were now due west, as well as due north, of us. The pine trees exploded one after another in showers of sparks and leaping flames, and we could not forget that the copse that has its southern tip within five yards of our outbuildings runs for some three hundred yards in a north-westerly direction. With the least change in the direction of the wind, our villa would become untenable.

My wife sensibly suggested that I should pack up a few valuables, since there would be no time to think of such things if the copse caught fire. I put into a suitcase my money, a few documents, the typescript of my latest book, and my only article of jewellery, a pair of gold cuff-links. Half way down the stairs, with the suitcase in one hand and my typewriter in the other, I paused, and turned back—there were three letters I had written just before the fireworks, and it seemed a pity to leave them to be burnt with everything else.

The flames, accompanied by loud crackling and explosions, marched on across our horizon and burnt themselves out. An expert tried to encourage me next day by assuring me that, since the wind had been strong, the individual trees would have been only superficially burnt, and would have a good chance of recovery. We should, perhaps, escape with nothing much worse than a blackened sky-line, and fresh vegetation would soon break through. We should, he said, have little cause for complaint—only three weeks previously, our friend and neighbour, Lionel Fielden, had seen his whole forest, just behind his villa, go up in smoke, partly because the fire-fighting arrangements around Lucca, despite the pine forests on most of its hills, are so poor. The forestry guards are hopelessly understaffed and, at least in some areas, are not even on the telephone. The fire brigade does not pay much attention to forest fires, and the army presumably has other things to do than to beat them out. Above all, as I have reluctantly pointed out elsewhere in this chapter, there is a sad lack of that civic sense which should lead automatically to concerted action in any village against so unselective a menace as fire.

So nobody seemed greatly to worry next day about the extent to which the burnt-out woods near us were still smouldering, and when we came back from a morning's shopping in Lucca I saw smoke rising between trees that had hitherto escaped damage. I decided that, after a short siesta, I would go up the hill to investigate. The siesta was very short. In no time at all, a very anxious Annunziata was knocking on the door to announce that the fire was very close to the house.

It wasn't, but it was certainly spreading our way, although the wind was still driving the flames and smoke in the other direction. I found Gino and Giuseppe sitting on a log in our copse and enjoying the spectacle—the fire, they had decided, was not a danger to us, and it did not seem to matter that it might be a danger to somebody else.

At any rate, I told them rather snappily, I was going to see for myself, and I began to climb the hill with a speed that

47

did not match my years. I had on my thickest and oldest shoes, the soles of which had worn very smooth, and the grass was so dry that it crackled like new snow after a very sharp frost. I slithered about, very conscious that the two Gs were probably chuckling at the old man's habit of interfering in business that was not strictly his own. When I came to the crest of the hill, I found half a dozen young men eating the grapes from a menaced vineyard. There was nothing else to do, they pointed out, and the two or three older men who were chopping down trees in the hope of making a firebreak were wasting their time; nothing could check the advance of the flames.

I refused to agree with them. I went on into the wood with a farmer I knew, each of us glad for the company of the other. We had to shout in order to be heard above the crackling and explosions of the fire in the undergrowth, and when one of the pine trees burst into sudden flames, twenty or thirty feet high, there was a roar as though a huge wave had crashed on to some beach. The hot air created a wind almost of gale force, in which burning branches shot up towards the sky. The farmer agreed with the younger men: there was nothing to be done.

Had anybody telephoned for the fire brigade? I asked. Apparently nobody had. Wasn't it the obvious thing to do? Nobody seemed to think so, and in any case, nobody but I had the telephone installed. They shrugged their shoulders. They were fatalists. They doubted whether the firemen would come unless some house were in grave danger. Besides, there was no water anywhere near which the firemen could use.

Angered by their passivity, I walked round to the leeward side of the wood. Despite the contrary breeze, the grass was so dry that the flames were advancing at least a yard a minute towards a copse of fine young trees. The firemen would at least know more about checking its advance than we did. I hurried down the hill again towards my house, and

I looked so red and angry that Giuseppe and Gino rose shamefacedly to their feet. By the time I had telephoned, they had fetched axes, and they accompanied me up the hill again. The copse was already burning. 'You could have saved that,' I told them angrily, although both they and I knew that they could have done nothing of the kind.

Below the copse, the ground had once been terraced for olives, and a path of sorts ran along one of these terraces. Here, by 'back-burning', and thus making a firebreak, we managed to check the flames, beating them out with branches every time they crossed the gap we had made. The heat was so intense that we could beat down the flames for only a few seconds at a time, and when I retired to get my breath in the cooler air, Annunziata, a great respecter of routine, came up to me. It was tea-time, she announced. What should she do about it? With some difficulty, I refrained from telling her in very vulgar language.

The firemen arrived, and turned the scale in our favour. They advised us where we could safely leave the flames to burn themselves out, because the harm they had done was so great that they could do no more. We stood around self-consciously and rather proud of ourselves. The fire brigade chief wanted to know who had telephoned, and I came forward for his congratulations. He was more interested, I discovered, in getting my name and address, since there might be a bill for his services. (In the event, there wasn't.) I overheard a discussion about the owner of a small part of the wood and the frequency with which he sent in claims to the insurance company for damage done by fires. Had I been interfering, I wondered, with a recognized way in which a poor farm-worker could get a little money from a rich company? My pride took another tumble when, for the first time, I looked down the hill below our fire-break— there were two indifferent rows of pines and then several bramble-covered terraces that would certainly have been better for a burning. A third blow came when I realized that the poplars on the floor of the valley were not the ones that mark the borders of my land; my own were a hundred yards further away from the fire than I had realized.

Two days later, I walked again over the area. In the vineyard that ran down one side of the wood, the grapes had been roasted a shiny brown, and tasted beastly. The blackened tree trunks had been stippled most attractively with delicate white ash. Here and there, smoke still rose from the ground, but I found that in each case it came from round holes at the bottom of which was all that remained of large trees. The holes were so deep that probably the smouldering wood at the bottom of them was not at all dangerous. Out of curiosity, rather than with a praiseworthy determination to extinguish the fire, I urinated into one of these craters. Up came a cloud of steam reminiscent, in a very small and humble way, of what happens when one pours a bucketful of water on the hot stones of a Finnish *sauna*. Less than a minute later, an impertinent little flame reappeared. Perhaps I ought, after all, to fetch some water? But my sense of duty deserted me. 'Oh hell!' I said to myself, 'it's not my job to put out fires on somebody else's land.' But I was a little ashamed by my lack of civic responsibility, and I was very relieved when I looked out of the attic window that evening, and could see no smoke creeping up between the blackened tree-trunks.

# Chapter Two

I HAD been so glad to get Gino to run my small farm that I had not paid enough attention to the other members of his family—his wife, Maria, and his daughter, Giulietta. It was enough for me that Maria was sister to Annunziata; so honest, if also so untidy. But the difference between the sisters, and between husband and wife, was extraordinary. Gino created a favourable impression by his obvious and jovial good humour, but an unfavourable one by his gaping trousers and his greyish vest, rotted into holes by his honest sweat. Maria looked far more like a duchess than any duchess I have ever met—and, living in Italy, where titles are inherited by all the children and where popes and emperors competed for centuries in winning loyalties by the distribution of these honours, one is likely to meet a good many of them. Dressed in suitable clothes, she would find it far less difficult than Eliza Doolittle to enter the highest ranks of snobbish society, for her natural good manners match her physical beauty. After her arrival at the *podere*, she became stouter and more matronly, but this change merely added to the majesty of her appearance, which derived partly from the bone structure of her face, but even more from an inner, religious calm that was increased, rather than diminished, by the sorrows that she has had to face since she came to live as our nearest neighbour.

Giulietta was the only child of Maria and Gino, and we were at first a little disturbed to learn that there was to be this girl of twenty; the Italians are as impervious to noise as the Chinese, and we feared that there would be rowdy parties of young people in the *contadino*'s cottage, separated from ours only by a long pergola covered by vines. We were told that she would leave home on her motor-cycle each morning at half past five to work in a local factory, but she might nevertheless make the evenings hideous with the latest pop music from the loudest of transistors. Then we were told that she was engaged to be married, which meant either that she would leave her factory after her marriage or would leave her infants (for there would certainly be no pill in so deeply Catholic a household) to her mother to look after, to the detriment of our *podere*.

Our fears were unnecessary. Giulietta was as beautiful as her mother, but, despite her great beauty, she was quiet, modest and gentle. During her holidays, she enjoyed passing the dishes round if we had guests for a meal, and I learnt quite a lot about the characters of these guests by observing how much attention they paid to her instead of to the food she was serving. She bore no resemblance to the unwashed, unkempt and undisciplined girls, mostly from northern Europe, who hitch-hike along the Italian *autostrade* from spring to autumn. Indeed, she was so demure that she reminded me of the daughter of an Italian doctor in whose family I had lived near Florence more than half a century ago. But few things about Italy have impressed me more than the contrast between the freedom granted to Giulietta and the absence of freedom granted to Luisina.

When Giulietta's own Vespa was out of order, nobody thought it strange that she should ride pillion behind Giancarlo, her *fiancé*. With him, she was allowed to wander at will about our fields and through our copse. Luisina, on the other hand, was never allowed out alone, and was so protected in the house by her mother or by the fat German *Fraülein* that I was never left alone with her. As soon as I came into the sitting-room, Luisina would walk out of it, as though I were suffering from an infectious disease (which, I suppose, calf love is).

*　*　*

This conversion of a pleasant Italian sitting-room into an

isolation ward was all the more painful to me because I had come to Italy from a small town in West Prussia, now part of Poland, where I had enjoyed a freedom that must have been exceptional at that time. I had lived for six months with a German family, where—as one is apt to do at seventeen—I had developed a deathless passion, first, for the younger daughter and, later, for her sister. This passion I recorded in my diary, and, in 1929, I expanded the record into a book. Thirty-seven years later, Philip Purser turned this book, *Calf Love*, most brilliantly into a television play for the B.B.C., and thereby gave me one of my strangest emotional experiences.

Being in Italy, I missed both broadcasts of Purser's play, but a special showing of it was put on for my benefit at the Television Centre on my next visit to London. There I sat, between Simon Ward, who had been me in the play, and Isobel Black, who had been Friedel, and through them I was reliving events that had happened more than fifty years earlier. Isobel Black bore no physical resemblance to Friedel —for one thing, she was very much prettier—and Simon Ward bore no resemblance to me—for one thing, he was much better-looking. But the emotions they expressed were those that Friedel and I had expressed so many years before; Simon *was* me and Isobel *was* Friedel, and yet there *I* was, sitting between them in the Television Centre. Hardened old sinner though I am, I felt for this girl, some fifty years my junior, the same almost religious adoration that had ended so disastrously for me in Bromberg, before the First World War. For an hour or so, until we came out into the cold, rational atmosphere of London in November, I was the ghost, revisiting Bromberg, Provinz Posen, in the summer of 1911.

I was, I think, the only possessor of a British passport in Bromberg (and I possessed one only because I was not very far from Russia, one of the three or four countries for which a passport was required). Since I was English, and Englishmen are notoriously cold-blooded, I was allowed to go for excursions with Friedel into the pine forests that surrounded Bromberg. But, as bad luck would have it—or was it really good luck?—she was in love not with me, but with a medical student whose home was down the road. So I was expected to show my devotion by sneaking round to tell her beloved when and where we would meet him. The forest was carpeted with lilies of the valley, and even after nearly sixty years, their scent brings back to me the memory of my misery as I wandered alone among them, waiting until the time came for me to meet her again and to walk home sedately at her side.

Her lover was killed in the early days of the First World War, and I believe he died in that part of Flanders where I was discovering the discomforts of trench warfare. As far as I know, the only German I ever shot was a rather fat man walking along a communicating trench, unaware that we had dug a sniping post under the sandbags of our own trench. He wore no shirt and he carried a towel; he therefore appeared more like an ordinary human being on his way back from the bathroom than a bitter enemy of my country (which, most probably, he was not, any more than I was a bitter enemy of his). But there I was, the platoon commander with the privilege and duty of inaugurating our sniping post on Hill 60, and there he was, right in my line of fire. I shot him, but quite deliberatly I shot him in the arm, and I hope that I saved his life by sending him away from the firing line for several weeks or months. Had he been Friedel's medical student, as he might have been, should I have aimed differently? I don't think so. At times I had hated him, but generally I have felt a sympathy, or even an affection, for the boys or men who had the good taste to fall in love with the same girls or women as I did.

In my Bromberg days, they were far more tolerant than in most other parts of Europe. Whereas, later, I was not to be left a minute in a room alone with Luisina, only Friedel's suspicious old aunt protested because her niece was allowed to give me German lessons in the relative seclusion of the apple orchard. I have already suggested that society was especially permissive there because I was an Englishman. But it was permissible for any young girl and any young man to walk together along the Danzigerstrasse in the late afternoon, providing they both carried tennis rackets. The Danzigerstrasse was the *Bummelstrasse*—every German town had one—along which people strolled up and down, greeting acquaintances and collecting material for gossip, and gossip turned to scandal on the slightest excuse. But, however tight her skirt, a girl's reputation was saved by a tennis racket; it was evidence that she had been playing tennis, and the parents probably realised that no sexual disaster was likely to occur on a tennis court.

\* \* \*

Lucca's equivalent of a *Bummelstrasse* is the group of short, narrow streets near the open place that, some twenty centuries ago, was the Roman forum. The *ora del passeggio*, the time when everyone turns out for an evening stroll, is so

much a tradition that wheeled traffic is forbidden in these streets between sunset and night. The ancient forum is still crowded on two mornings a week with local farmers who meet to discuss their cows, their crops, their politics and other people's women much as their ancestors must have done when Julius Caesar was Proconsul of the city and when, according to Plutarch, Caesar, Pompey and Crassus met here to decide how they were going to divide between them the government of their great empire. (Their ambitions brought them to bad ends—Caesar, as everybody knows, was stabbed by political rivals; Pompey, fighting against his father-in-law—none other than Caesar himself—fled to Egypt, where Ptolemy, who had promised him protection, had him murdered as soon as he landed; Crassus was killed by a Parthian general who poured molten gold down his throat. It is encouraging thus to be reminded that our own century has not a monopoly of bloodshed and brutality.)

But the *passeggio* in Italy is not what it used to be. It is still an occasion for the young men to stare at the young girls and the young girls to show off to the young men, but 'wolf whistles' are no longer necessary, now that members of both sexes can stop and talk to each other without causing a single eyebrow to be raised in disapproval. The two sexes are still segregated in the village churches, but the Italian girls are as nearly naked on the beaches as are the girls from the European cold north and are as hysterically excited by the pop singers of the moment.

\* \* \*

Until the arrival of Berto and Nunzia, the predecessors of Gino and Maria, I had treated our small *podere* only as an interesting adjunct to our house. It was amusing and very satisfying to have eggs from our own fowls, logs from our own woods, wine from our own vineyard, olive oil from our own trees, milk from our own cow, honey from our own bees, fruit from our own orchard and flowers from our own garden. But there was the obvious danger that, despite the efforts of Giuseppe and the others, there would be less and less farm produce year by year, that our fields would grow more and more weeds, that I should become increasingly ashamed of the Tuscan retreat, of which I had written so boastfully. We must become mechanized.

That decision was a sensational one when I made it in 1965, for our region consisted almost entirely of farms that were very small and very poorly equipped. (Since 1965, things have changed considerably, and in summer, at any time of the day except between one and three in the afternoon, I can hear some machine beside our own at work in the fields.) In *Tuscan Retreat*, I had been apologetic about my cow because, in accordance with local custom, she never left her stall except when she was needed to drag the creaking old farm cart or to provide the motive power for the plough. Mechanization would rob her of these excursions; the wooden yoke that had pressed so heavily on the necks of so many submissive beasts would probably be polished up and sold as an antique curiosity to somebody who wanted to give a rustic appearance to his country cottage.

In this province of Lucca, more than ninety per cent of the farms are smaller than my own fifteen acres. This is due mainly to the traditional system of inheritance which leads to more and more fragmentation of land. But a glance at the map, revealing the great spine of the Apennines running down the centre of the country, explains why farming can prosper in very few areas, of which Lucca is not one. You soon cease to wonder why farm-workers drift to the factories at a rate of some 350,000 every year.

This migration to the cities is probably even more important from the social than from the economic point of view, as it was in England during the Industrial Revolution. The men who farm around me are, for the most part, still very poor. Until fairly recently, they had very little contact with money, for they could supply almost all their own needs, and their kind of farming was probably the most suitable for the country's geography. But with the coming of the motor-cycle and the TV set, ambitions have changed. To keep young men in agriculture, the best hope is the development of large-scale and highly-mechanized farming. But, side by side with the development of these large modern farms—a development that is only just beginning—there is an urgent need for buying and selling cooperatives to help the small, independent farmer, for any nation is impoverished, socially if not financially, if it is deprived of the sturdy independence of the man who grows his own grain, makes his own wine, milks his own cows, and tramps home at dusk over his own land.

The much-abused (and much misused) system of share-cropping known as the *mezzadria*, which is now fast disappearing in Italy, had many grave disadvantages, especially in the South, where so many large estates are run by bailiffs for the benefit of absentee owners. It gave the *mezzadro* too poor and too uncertain a return for his labour—generally about sixty per cent of the produce of the farm. But it had one possible source of satisfaction—the *mezzadro* had a greater sense of ownership, or participation, than he has now, when he lives secure, with a regular wage. At least half the crop of maize, at least half the wine fermenting in the vat, at least half the oil being crushed out of the olives at the *frantoio*, was his, and was the direct result of his labour. Certainly, neither Berto nor Gino could have lived on sixty per cent of the produce of my farm, but the sense of participation is necessary if men—and, still more, women—are to continue their hard and lonely lives on the farm. I judge my own success or failure as a farmer much less by the amount of money I make or lose than by the cheerfulness of the people who work for me.

Each year, I have a long discussion with Giuseppe about growing grain. I remember the clouds of oily smoke that rose from the superfluous wheat that was being burned on the plains outside Winnipeg before the last war, and I argue that it is silly to grow grain in our small fields. How, I ask, can we possibly compete with the produce of the wide wheat belt of North America, or even with that from the rich plains of France or the rather less rich ones of Germany? The ton or two of wheat we send down to the local mill cannot fetch a price that will repay us adequately for the seed, the fertilizer, the labour and the hire of the threshing machine.

But Giuseppe is ready with all the answers. We must have straw for the cow-shed, to which I reply that it would be cheaper to buy the stuff. But, says Giuseppe, there must be a proper rotation of crops—turnips, hay, clover, beans, maize and grain. To that argument I find it difficult to answer effectively, since I am really on his side. But, even if my answer were effective, I suspect that we should still have our few fields of wheat and oats, out of respect for a tradition to which the Italian farmer is deeply attached. And with some reason—the walled hill-towns of Tuscany are a reminder that Italy was for many centuries a country of small states, all too often at war with each other when they were not at war with some foreign invader. The farmers had no walls to protect them, and their descendants have inherited an instinctive determination to be as nearly self-supporting as possible.

My own arguments used to be slightly weakened by the reflection that, if we grew our own wheat, there was a better chance that Maria would find time to bake our own bread. Even though we could not be sure that the flour we fetched from the mill was ground from our own wheat, the bread that she made from it was as different from the bread we buy in the local store as the eggs of our free-run chickens are different from those produced by battery hens. Alas, she seldom had time to bake it, but when she did so, I generally found excuses for leaving my desk and going to watch her from the moment she opened the eighteenth-century kneading trough filled with flour. She mixed the yeast—a lump of dough she had left over from the last bread-making—with warm water, and poured it into a depression made in the flour. Then she covered it over with more flour and left it until the following morning, by which time the mixture had risen almost until it lifted the lid of the trough.

Early on that morning, I would see white smoke rising from the chimney of the bread oven as Maria packed it with faggots from the olive grove, the vine-yard or the copse. While the oven was getting hot, she would go next door to the bread trough where, with all precautions to keep out cold air, she poured a bucketful of hot water into the flour and began to knead it. She thrust her arms down through the heavy mass, turned it over, pushed it this way and that, for a full quarter of an hour. Then she cut off a large lump of dough, kneaded it afresh, and put it on a board on which she had sprinkled maize to prevent the loaves from sticking. Just before she covered each lump with a sheet, she made on it the sign of the cross (as I believe many people who are not Catholics do in other countries). When all the future loaves had been thus blessed and covered over with a blanket, she left them for an hour and returned to the bread oven.

With cabbage leaves tied to a long pole, she swept aside the charcoal, and the loaves were pushed into the oven on a flat, wooden spade which she withdrew with a sharp jerk, leaving a row of large blobs of dough which the miracle of heat would turn into fresh, crisp loaves of bread. And the smell when she opened the oven door was so delicious that I rank it with those other delicious smells of tar, of roasting coffee, and of new-mown hay.

Delicious, and also evocative. When I stood in the shed as Maria took the loaves out of the oven, this smell carried me back a long, long way—back, in fact, to the year 1900. I was busy in the baker's shop in Charminster, kneading flour for the small loaf that the baker allowed me to make once a week, when I was told that they were forming a procession to celebrate the relief of Mafeking. I already knew about Mafeking, since my earliest exercise in reporting had been to go round to the local printer each day immediately after lunch to copy down the news bulletin that he stuck up in his window. I knew that Mafeking's relief was very important, although I had no idea what 'relief' meant in this context. But that ignorance, of course, did not affect my desire to take part in the procession, and I ran up the hill to where it was being formed, outside the cottage inhabited by an old lady with the first talking parrot I had ever met—I've forgotten the old lady, but I still can remember the plumage of the parrot.

As the smallest participant in the procession, I was given a Union Jack nailed to a pole. Half-way down the hill was the old house in which I was staying with my Cousin Honor. She stood on the doorstep by the side of Aunt Bessie, sitting very upright in her wheeled chair, with her lace cap perched on her head. How proud they would both be of me, I thought, marching along with a flag. The shock was all the greater when I saw that Cousin Honor was frowning and making angry signals, from which I gathered that I was trailing the Union Jack in the dust. I was not tall enough to hold the flag as high as it should have been held, and for the rest of the march down to the church I suffered agonies of humiliation because I was too small and too weak to be worthy of my great responsibility. I was silent and sad in a crowd where everybody else sang or shouted with an excitement that has given undesirable immortality to the little South African town.

\* \* \*

The decision to buy a tractor was not fulfilled for several months, partly because money was scarce, but even more because none of us knew anything at all about mechanized agriculture. Giuseppe goes everywhere on his Vespa, which he rides with far more care than I should have expected—the fact that Annunziata crosses herself before she clambers on to the pillion seat is, I think, rather a habit than an indica-

tion of distrust in her husband. Gino had a less lethal machine, a cross between a pedal cycle and a motor-cycle, on which he had no licence to pay although its power to damage pedestrians was still formidable. But neither Gino nor Giuseppe had ever driven a machine with four wheels.

We went over to a display of agricultural machinery organized by the Shell Agricultural Centre at Borgo a Mozzano, an ancient little town in the mountains north of Lucca, in which one meets people of every colour and speaking a fantastic variety of languages (since the Shell Company organizes courses there for agricultural officers from every part of the world). For an hour or so, we watched machines at work, while their salesmen thrust into our hands leaflets with gay illustrations of enthusiastic families welcoming Pop as he drove some machine to the front door (but none of Pop paying the bills). The various technical terms left the three of us bewildered. I drove away in a mood of such depression over the new responsibilities I was planning to accept that even Gino's backchat with Giuseppe failed to amuse me.

The next morning, I went up to the three cypress trees that mark the northern limit of our *podere*. To the west of me, in the great bowl formed by the Apuan Alps and the Pisan Hills, the towers of Lucca were shining in the sun. In front, rising above the contorted branches of my olives, were the forest-covered slopes of Monte Serra. Away to the east, on a spur of this mountain, stood the little town of Castelvecchio di Compito, as white and withdrawn from the world as some hill town in the Moorish part of Spain. This view is, I think, as lovely as any view could be that does not include the sea. But near at hand, on either side of my *podere*, were the reminders of my dilemma—olive orchards in which the strength of the roots was all wasted in useless shoots; vineyards in which the vines were being ousted by the brambles; terraces which were crumbling in decay. I had bought this place with very little thought about its agricultural aspect— the great casks in the *cantina* had fascinated me, but I had not taken them very seriously; the fields had meant little more than an attractive precaution against builders who would otherwise come along and spoil my view by putting up the ugly modern houses that desecrate so much of the Italian countryside. But now I had to decide whether I was to let my land go slowly out of production, like the land around us, or whether I was to be worthy of the labour contributed by Gino and Giuseppe in their effort to make the *podere* as tidy and as productive as it had probably been before the seven lean years of neglect that had preceded our purchase of it. (I know that I hark back to this problem elsewhere in this book: I was, and have been until fairly recently, obsessed by my feeling of responsibility towards this Italian hillside.)

'I'm afraid we shall have to do without that tractor,' I said to Gino.

'As you decide. We've still got the cow, the cow and me. We'll manage all right.' He laughed about it, but I realized how disappointed he had been by the way his face brightened when I told him I was going into Lucca that very morning to ask advice at the *Consorzio Agrario* about the best machine to buy.

Each Italian province has an official *Consorzio Agrario*, which exists to stimulate good farming. I take my wine there to be analysed. I buy my seed and fertilizers from its shop. When I am lucky, I get an expert to come out to the *podere* to advise me how to solve my problems. The Italian government does little to help agriculture but at any rate as far as the *Consorzio Agrario* is concerned in our province, it deserves all praise. I have had nothing but friendly help from its officials—possibly they are so accustomed to landowners who abandon their farms that they are over-pleased to find some poor fool who actually buys a small *podere* and hopes to make a success of it.

With the help of the *Consorzio Agrario*, and a government loan at a low rate of interest which the *Consorzio* negotiated on my behalf, I bought a *motocoltivatore*, a nice little tractor that chugs around the farm. But that, I found, was only the beginning—there were all the attachments one buys, or resists the temptation to buy. We had some hopes of planting a new vineyard, and there is a machine that will dig the yard-deep hole needed for each vine. We have two copses that would look so much better and would be so much healthier if we had a mechanical saw with which to thin them out. There is a machine that sprays the olives and the vines, and would spare Giuseppe the task of walking up and down the rows with a heavy spraying tank on his back. There is a machine that would pump water out of our pond, another that would mow the hay, another that would sow seed in nice straight rows, and another that would spread manure. There were such good arguments in favour of each of these and of several others that I was as tempted as any woman visiting a bargain basement. Only the prices of the articles were not bargain basement prices.

In the end, a lorry arrived with the tractor, a truck, a plough and a mower. And also a man to explain to Gino how everything worked. (He addressed Gino because he was the *contadino*, but one knew that Giuseppe would soon take over.) Gino in the saddle was as excited as a small boy with his first toy tricycle. With the mechanic on one side of him and Giuseppe on the other, each shouting instructions or advice at the top of his voice, he became so confused and flustered that at one moment I feared he would give up, and say he could never learn. But fortunately the excitement was a little stronger than the bewilderment, and before dusk he was teaching Giuseppe and me, and offering free rides to his daughter, Giulietta.

Gino's moment of glory was short-lived. He deferentially vacated the seat on the tractor for me, and I enjoyed pulling the truck laden with manure down to the maize field, or with olive faggots back to the farm. But before I was used to the machine, he invited me to take my turn at the plough.

With one wheel in the deep furrow, the tractor leant over at a preoccupying angle and, at the furrow's end, I was too confused to pull almost simultaneously at one lever to change gear and at another to lift the plough. Giuseppe was less reluctant than Gino to tell me what I had done wrong, and he quickly replaced me in the driving seat. I drove my first car—an air-cooled Humberette—in 1915, but the speed and impulsiveness of Italian drivers are sapping my self-confidence, and I used to hope that Giuseppe would take over the steering wheel of my own car, but that hope has long-since been dispelled—he becomes so completely tongue-tied in the presence of officialdom that he could never get a driving-licence. But the tractor had no terrors for him; once I had decided that my schoolboy desire to control this noisy and powerful machine was smaller than my fear of being humiliated by it, he took over.

Gino was hurt; he, too, would have liked to drive and, as *contadino* in charge of the farm, it was surely his job to do so? I freely admitted that it was. But Giuseppe had been engaged to look after the house, the garden, the outbuildings and the wine; only his good nature and his desire to see the *podere* prosper brought him out day after day and for hour after hour into the fields. He had a passion for playing with the tractor, I said in a tone that almost suggested to Gino that he and I were too grown-up for such enjoyments, and the important thing was that the *podere* benefited from this passion. So Gino, who was too gentle to want to be leader, kept busy with spade or scythe while Giuseppe sat hour after hour on the tractor's bumpy and uncomfortable seat.

Gino's regrets tended to disappear when the tractor pulled the harrow. Our soil in summer acquires an almost rock-like hardness, and the harrow by itself is too light to break up the clumps of earth. We weighed it down with great slabs of rock, but even that was not enough. It became effective only when Gino added his fifteen stone. He stood on a board lashed to the top of the harrow, and carried out remarkable feats of balancing; one had only to catch his eye to know how greatly he was enjoying himself.

He had one other phase of authority, and that came during the *vendemmia*. Ever since I bought the farm, Giuseppe has been in charge of the wine-making, and that kept him all day in the dark *cantina*, but Gino was in charge of picking the grapes, and that kept him out all day in the sunshine, supervising his small team of pickers. Before we became mechanized, this job was less important than now, for our old cow could pull only about a quarter of the load we put in the truck. Once we had become mechanized, there was no delay while the farm cart creaked its way back to the *cantina* with its *bigonci* piled high with grapes—a *bigoncio* being one of the chestnut tubs, placed here and there along the line of vines, into which we empty our baskets or buckets. Instead, there was a large vat in the truck, and a preliminary crushing, with the help of a thick wooden pole, took place on the spot. This left Gino with the kind of challenge he enjoyed: one moment he was picking—and only when I picked on one side while he picked on the other did I realize how much skill and speed are involved—then Maria, or some friend who had volunteered to help, would call out that the nearest *bigoncio* was full, and he would hurry away to empty it. However much I might hope for a minute's rest because my basket was full, Gino found time to replace it by an empty one on his way back to the tractor. As soon as the vat was full and all our baskets were more or less empty, Gino would drive off to the *cantina*, where he poured the juice into a press perched across the top of the large vat, while Giuseppe turned a handle like the handle of a giant barrel-organ. No more than a very short gossip before Gino, knowing that our baskets would be full again, would leave the uncomplaining Giuseppe to do both jobs—to pour the must into the press and to turn the handle to complete the preliminary crushing of the grapes, in readiness for the fermentation to begin under the crust of pips, skins and stalks.

I have already written about the arguments between Giuseppe, from Pisa, and Berto, the *contadino*, from Lucca. Gino, like Berto, was a Lucchese, but he was too good-tempered and too lacking in jealousy to argue for long. The arguments, if they deserve so pejorative a word, are now between Giuseppe and myself, and they have led both to my greatest triumph and my greatest humiliation.

Before I began to interfere, Giuseppe made his wine in the traditional Italian way. The black grapes, with their skins, stalks and pips, went into one vat, to bubble away for ten days or so until the first fermentation was over; the white grapes, also with their skins, stalks and pips, went into another. Only when this fermentation had ended, did we empty the vats and pour the resulting liquids—dark red in the first case, muddy yellow in the second—into the barrels to become wine by the time the winter was over. But to my mind, this process had two disadvantages. Our vines know no colour segregation—those producing black grapes are mixed up with those producing white grapes, and the work of picking them would be very much lighter if Giuseppe did not decree that one day we should pick only white grapes and another, only black grapes. Since all the colour is in the skins, why not make our white wine *alla francese*, in the French way, by crushing the grapes all together and then immediately siphoning off as much juice as we needed for our white wine into casks, where it could ferment gently and at leisure? In the second place, white wine made *alla francese*, and separated as soon as possible from the skins and pips, would have less of the roughness I dislike (but Giuseppe likes) about so many Italian wines.

I suspect that Giuseppe, on election days, cancels Annunziata's Christian Democrat vote by himself voting Communist. Only once have I heard him call upon God, and that was the day when I first made this suggestion. God, he assured me, made white grapes for white wine and black grapes for red wine (or black wine, as the *contadini* prefer to call it, and the more unscrupulous wine merchants add ox blood and other materials to give it a darker, richer colour). He hinted that it would be sacrilegious to break this unwritten law. He has heard of champagne (although he has never tasted it), and he knows that it costs a lot of money, and it was only when I showed him an Italian book which mentioned that most champagne is made of black grapes that he began to waver.

He still argued. I had to admit that the use of black grapes to make white wine was more dangerous than the normal Italian way of using only white grapes and letting their juice ferment in a vat with their pips and stalks and skins, for the stalks contain tannin, and without tannin the wine will not keep or improve; indeed, it may develop an illness known as 'the yellows', and lose its flavour. Also, the acid content is likely to be low, and acid—horrible in the finished product —helps the wine to resist disease. Against such arguments, I insisted that the resulting wine should have a much more delicate flavour, but Giuseppe is much less interested in delicacy than in strength. In the end, he agreed, very reluctantly, that we should fill one barrel with this Frenchified white wine, and it was still untapped and untested when I wrote *Tuscan Retreat*.

On the day when we planned to tap this barrel, it seemed that about half the village—quite by chance, of course,—came up to the villa. One man wanted to borrow a scythe; another brought back one of our ladders; another had some question about one of our cows; another wondered if we had any spare hay for sale. They all drifted into the *cantina*.

I was nervous, for my reputation was at stake. But my nervousness was nothing compared with Giuseppe's. I was merely an eccentric Englishman, known to give good quality meat to my cats and to oppose the mass shooting of small birds; he was a professional wine-maker, with generations of tradition to warn him against foolish foreign experiments. Hesitatingly, he turned the spigot, and out flowed a clear white wine, paler than a white Burgundy and deliciously fresh to the taste. From that day onward, Giuseppe seems to have forgotten that he has not made wine *alla francese*, with a predominance of black grapes ever since he was a boy, and he shares my feeling of triumph every time a local farmer tells us he is making wine in the same way. (This does happen, although, I admit, it does not happen often.)

But I am still not convinced that he is fully converted to my belief that the grapes normally used to make the rather rough red wine of the Chianti country can turn into a light, fresh and very agreeable white wine. I missed a recent *vendemmia* because I was away in South Africa, writing a book about the colour problem—my last effort to reform the world—and as soon as I came home in the following March he poured out a very pale white wine. I tasted it almost with reluctance, for it could not possibly equal the white wines of South Africa, which have improved so much in the last twenty years that I drink them as joyfully as I drink the wines of the Mosel or of Alsace. What should I be able to say to Giuseppe that would conceal my disappointment?

I need not have worried. The wine was delicious, and new enough to be slightly sparkling. I told him so in what are called 'no uncertain terms', and he was delighted. 'This year,' he told me—and I thought I detected a note of triumph in his voice—'we made it *alla francese*, but using only white grapes.'

Secretly, I felt humiliated and a little annoyed, for I am still obsessed by this idea of making white wine out of black grapes, and of alleviating the task of picking, since all the grapes, whatever their colour, can be put into the same *bigonci*. But a few months later Giuseppe was honest enough to give me my revenge. He was having difficulty, he told me, in selling our white wine—the local buyers found it too pale!

\*    \*    \*

From this adventure of *vino alla francese*, we went on to the making of *vin rosé*, a little sweet to drink at table, but, well-chilled, a very pleasant drink before lunch on a hot day and certainly less harmful than your gins and tonic or your Camparis and soda. Most of the *vin rosé* on the market is the result of blending red wine and white wine, and I was shocked to read that this method was accepted even by André Simon, surely the greatest of all writers about wines since George Saintsbury, although he did condemn 'another sort of pink wine, which is merely any kind of white wine—except the best—with just enough cochineal added to it to make it blush'. Our *vin rosé* belongs proudly to the minority. In our small *cantina*, we should be ashamed to make it by a skilful blending of black and white wines; we make it from black grapes, the juice of which is separated from the skins before they have had time to give it too strong a colour and before the full fermentation has set in. This gives rise to a lot of friendly discussion between Giuseppe and myself as to when that right moment has arrived—a decision that is difficult to reach, since much of the pink tinge disappears while the must is fermenting slowly in the casks.

Our experiments went, I think, a little to our heads. We made—and still make, if I am there at the time—some white wine out of black grapes, a process fairly common in France, where it is known as *blanc de rouges*, but most uncommon in Italy. And we received one year an order for seventy gallons of our white wine from friends in Milan, which was a much greater event than one might imagine. We make nearly a thousand gallons a year and, until this Milan order stimulated our ambitions, we had sold most of it locally—at first to a local merchant, until I found out that he diluted our pure wine with stuff that might not even be wine at all, and then sold it as our wine to local farm workers who know that our wine is at least pure. After this discovery, we have always sold it direct to the consumer—although I reckon that one or two of them should, by now, have died of cirrhosis of the liver if they drank it all themselves.

Possibly some of them sell it at a profit, by the simple but dishonourable process of '*sofisticazione*', which means sophistication in its earlier English sense—it's no longer derogatory to tell someone that he's sophisticated. Wine in Italy that is 'sofisticato' may contain not only ox blood to darken it, but fish flour, seaweed, industrial alcohol and other substances that have no connection with the grape. Even Parmesan grated cheese, without which no good Italian can enjoy his soup or his *spaghetti*, may contain sawdust—and he eats nearly thirty kilogrammes of spaghetti or other forms of *pastasciutta* a year, as against the Englishman's less than half a kilogramme. The Italians drink more than twenty-five gallons of wine per head during the year (but very few of them get drunk); it is possible that some of my customers for wine pass it on to other customers in a slightly sophisticated form, but even so I expect that it is still purer than much of the stuff they would otherwise buy in elegant flasks or bottles.

If distant Milan thought it worth while to buy our wine, said Giuseppe to himself one day, it must be pretty good. I found him struggling with the machine that puts corks into bottles, and which I had not seen him using before, since such wine as we sell in flasks normally has a thin layer of olive oil, instead of a cork, to make it air-tight. The fermentation had scarcely begun and the water was fizzling noisily in the fermentation valve with which we replace the bung in the casks—on the principle of an Arab's hookah pipe, this valve allows the bubbles of carbonic acid gas to escape, but prevents the air, with all its unwanted and dangerous yeasts, from reaching the wine. Why, I asked him, was he putting new wine into old bottles. He replied proudly that he was making champagne and, in the absence of wire, he tied the corks down with the strongest cord he could find in the village store. I pointed out that champagne bottles had to be unusually strong and thick, but Giuseppe comforted me by saying that, if the fermentation were to become too violent—as it did in several cases—the cord would be more likely to break than the bottles.

It must have been some eighteen months later that I remembered our 'champagne' (I put the word in quotes, since champagne is made in only one small area of France, and in any case we could not attempt the very skilful process of *remuage* and *dégorgement* by which the deposit collects on the bottom of the cork, and is removed by an expert who changes corks almost with the speed of light). It was a hot day, and my guests welcomed the idea of drinking a chilled San Ginese sparkling wine. But when I took up a bottle to open it, I realised for the first time the vital importance of the large knob at the top of a champagne cork; how, without it, could I possibly open the bottle? The pressure of the imprisoned gas had, of course, swollen the lower end of the cork so that no corkscrew could pull it out.

With considerable disquiet, and with a towel wrapped round the bottle, I struggled with that cork until it began to crumble. Suddenly, the remains of it shot out of the bottle with a tremendous explosion. But the change of temperature and the violent treatment of the bottle while I had been trying to uncork it had the result that the cork was followed in the fraction of a second by a jet of wine, leaving us with nothing but the rather murky dregs. The force of the liquid must have been nearly equivalent to that of the water from fire hoses with which angry demonstrators are scattered by police. The bottles have now disappeared from the wine cellar, and I have not liked to ask Giuseppe what has happened to them.

\* \* \*

Champagne, above all other drinks, is associated with cheerful occasions. Not so much in my case. I am assured that half a pint at midday is highly to be recommended, but few of us can afford it. On occasions when I have drunk it, it has given me far more hangovers than happiness, and I admit that I would far prefer a white Burgundy or a Mosel (even if this admission puts me in the category of the comedian—

name long since forgotten—who used to confide to his audience that 'I don't believe in all this 'ere kissing; what I likes
is a nice 'ot cup of cocoa'). And on one occasion, champagne
made me acutely unhappy.

My father, one of ten children, had to abandon his ambition to become a doctor and to go into a bank. By way of
consolation, he became ambitious on my behalf instead. He
and my mother made great sacrifices—much greater sacrifices than I realized at the time—to send me to a public
school, and then to various foreign countries, in the hope that
I should one day become a consul, and spend much of my
time bailing drunken British sailors out of jail. The First
World War intervened before I had been humiliated by a
failure to pass the exam, and even before the war was over I
broke the news to my father that I was determined to earn
my living by writing.

'But what sort of a living?' he asked, with a mixture of
anxiety and reproach. He never reminded me of the way in
which he had saved money to help me towards a safe and
successful career, but his distress was obvious and very under-
standable. Nor was it lessened when I told him, a year before
the armistice, that I had risen from a reporter's job on the
*Daily Mail* at £3 a week to a sub-editor's job at Reuter's at
£4 10s 0d and that, with such a good income, I was about
to get married.

Well, luck was on my side. Things went well for me, and
one indication of this was a lecture I gave in the very early
days of the Second World War in Bournemouth, where he
was living in retirement. The meeting was undeniably a
success (mainly, I suspect, because I gave so many convinc-
ing reasons why Hitler was certain to be defeated) and my
father was obviously proud and delighted when a few
friends came round to his house after it was over. He appeared
suddenly with a bottle of champagne. 'This ought to be
good,' he assured us. 'It's one of three bottles old Colonel
Meredith gave me years ago. We drank one bottle on my

sixtieth birthday, and one on the day of my retirement from the bank. I've been keeping this last bottle for some very special occasion, and there won't be any better occasion than this.'

The guests made the usual polite noises and I tried to look modest. I offered to open the bottle for him, but he waved me aside. He wrapped a napkin round the neck of the bottle and, with great caution, undid the wire. Amid expressions of alarm from the ladies, he began to work the cork from side to side. And, as he did so, I experienced a sudden anxiety for him that amounted almost to fear.

For Colonel Meredith, I reflected, must have died at least twenty years ago, and most probably the champagne had been in his cellar for several years before his death. How many years would normally elapse before the wine lost its life, its sparkle? Surely not more than two decades? I tried to remember everything I had ever read about champagne, but before I could reach any conclusion the cork came out, noiselessly and without vigour, and the liquid that my father poured into the glass he had placed with such strategic care was deep yellow in colour, and quite lifeless. He stood there, the bottle in one hand and the napkin in the other, and with an expression of such pathetic surprise on his face that I felt my eyes fill with tears of affection for this saddened old man.

\* \* \*

The failure of our own effort to make sparkling wine did not deprive Giuseppe of further ambitions. Why, he asked me one morning, did we not send some of our wine to England where, he understood, they made no wine themselves. I confess that I was strongly tempted. One early name for my land was Corte Salome (why, nobody has been able to explain), and I should like to see on my club wine list '*Vino Bianco di San Ginese, Corte Salome*' or something of that sort. My vanity would be immensely flattered, as it has been by the few prizes won by my cows at the cattle show, although in both cases my satisfaction is illogical, the only achievement that can genuinely please me being something connected with this business of writing. On my next visit to London two wine merchants offered to take what, I believe, is known in the trade as a 'parcel'. I had seen Osbert Sitwell's excellent wine from the Chiantigiana listed in London; why not mine?

But to make the experiment worth while, I should need to plant some thousands of young vines to fill the gaps, wider and wider each year, in my vineyard, and I should have to wait at least four years before the young vines began to produce. Four years, at my time of life? I found myself hesitating. It was all very well to talk grandiloquently about improving the output of the *podere*, but there were so many other ways of improving it which would show a quicker return for my capital and the *contadino*'s labour. Our south-western slopes are particularly good for vines. The great empty cask in the *cantina* was a bulky reminder that the *podere* had at one time produced much more wine than it produced today. But I had to admit that there was some dishonesty about my proclaimed desire to serve the land. I want to serve it, but I would also like to see the results of my service. I turned Giuseppe's attention to other matters.

I am still fascinated by the mystery of fermentation which turns the sugar of the grape into alcohol. (The Italians say the wine is 'boiling' when it ferments; the Romans used to say '*fermentat*' about some liquid that began to boil.) I cannot resist the temptation to climb the ladder at the side of the vat and to break through the crust of stalks, pips and skins with the heavy pole that Giuseppe keeps there for the purpose. This should be done at least twice a day; if the crust hardens, and the carbon dioxide cannot escape, the wine will get diseased. I break through the crust more often than is necessary, even though I am well aware of the dangers contained in that delicious vinous smell that I release. Philip M. Wagner, my most helpful guide in the matter of wine-making, warns me that the fermenting wine releases so much carbon dioxide that 'people have been suffocated to death by the gas. . . . Persons entering a poorly-ventilated fermenting cellar when violent fermentation is under way usually carry a lighted candle, which goes out if the gas is too thick for safety'.*

A lighted candle? I try to picture Giuseppe's expression if I were to appear candlestick in hand; and I run the risk of suffocation, just as I run all kinds of other risks to the wine because we fall so far short of Wagner's antiseptic American standards of cleanliness in our *cantina*. His warnings remind me of the small American boy who once came to lunch with us when we were living in the middle of an orange orchard in Cyprus, and who refused a delicious orange drink because it had not come out of a bottle.

\* \* \*

My former colleague on the *News Chronicle*, Lord Ritchie Calder, wrote some years ago in *Wine Mine†* about an imaginary professor who tries to 'explain' alcohol. 'Eyeing his goblet as though it were a retort, he lucubrates: "Yeast contains an enzyme, pyruvic carboxylase, which splits a molecule of carbon dioxide from pyruvate, thereby forming acetaldehyde. The acetaldehyde then reacts with DPNH to form ethyl-alcohol and DPN, in the presence of another enzyme called dehydrogenase." '

All this, no doubt, makes sense to the expert. I recognize most of the words, for they appear in every book on wine in that chapter which I plan to study sometime, and never shall. From L. W. Marrison's excellent Penguin book, *Wines and Spirits*, I learn that one of the principal functions of enzymes is to convert the starch in the vine into the sugar in the grape, as they also convert into sugar the starch in our bodies. 'A single yeast cell, which is about one five-thousandth

---

\* *American Wines and Wine-Making* (Alfred Knopf, New York, 1933).
† Published quarterly by Messrs. Peter Dominic, Horsham.

of an inch across, may contain a thousand different enzymes.'

But, lest you feel contempt for such small organisms, Marrison goes on to say that 'a single drop of an extract of rennin, one of the enzymes of rennet, will curdle four tons of milk in ten minutes'. The boiling and bubbling of the grape juice during fermentation, which causes me to lean for longer than is wise over the edge of our vat, is only the enzyme carboxylase acting on the pyruvic acid to drive out the carbon dioxide. What remains is acetaldehyde, which may easily turn into vinegar, but which, with the help of yet another enzyme, will turn into the wine I am lucky enough to drink every day. It's all so simple, or it would be if somebody could explain it to me in terms that would enable me to explain it to Giuseppe. But fortunately he does his job without any idea of his dependence upon the thousand different enzymes to be found in a single yeast cell.

With Ritchie Calder, 'I prefer to believe in yeast as a sacred mystery and to hold, with the Ancient Egyptians, that the secret of alcohol was the gift of the God Osiris to his wife, Isis, four thousand years ago. Or, more likely, it was the gift of Isis to Osiris, because it is my contention that fermentation and alcohol were discovered in the kitchen by women, although they have been disclaiming it ever since.'

We all know about Noah, who 'drank wine and was drunken', and about the punishment meted out to his son, Ham—a punishment that seems unduly harsh in these permissive days. But we do not know if or when Noah really lived. Ritchie Calder writes, however, that 'yeasts probably have as early an origin as the bacteria. Fossil evidence shows budding fungi in the Devonian Period, 320,000,000 years ago. . . . In their natural state, those [yeasts] concerned with fermentation pass the winter in the soil, and are disseminated by bees, dust and other agencies in the spring. In the case of fruits, the yeast dusts attach themselves to the skins, and the earliest date-wine in Egypt was prepared by pressing the liquid from soaked dates and leaving the juice to be fer-

mented by the wild yeast introduced by the date skins.'
Dr Michael Grant* reckons that the Egyptians first imported
vines soon after Egypt had become a single kingdom—
somewhere about the twenty-fifth century B.C.—and in due
course they specialized, 'with labels defining *clos*, year,
vintner and quality. Grape seeds found in early tombs closely
resemble species still extensively cultivated today.' Various
alcoholic drinks were filtered into jars by the Egyptians,
closed with clay stoppers, and sealed. 'Proprietary names in
Egypt included "The Joy-Bringer", "The Beautiful-Good"
and "The Draught of Heaven".' Not so very far, except in
time, from my own 'Corte Salome'.

* * *

In the early spring, before the weather gets too warm, we
rack our wine. On one day in early March, with the sun
blazing outside, I suggested to Giuseppe that we should
begin the process, and he was politely reproachful. Did I not
realise that the moon was waxing, and that, if we were to
change the wine from one cask to another at that state of
the moon, it would be thick and turgid? No less an expert
than Edward Hyams, who has the courage to make wine
from his own grapes in a Dartmoor valley, assures me that
there is no evidence to support such a superstition. But is it
only a superstition? Since it is obvious that the moon has so
strong a pull on the oceans as to create tides, is it impossible
that it draws up the lees from the bottom of a cask? After all,
a French wine taken to the southern hemisphere becomes
cloudy at the same seasons as it would in the vineyards
where it originated; it remembers its ancestry. Anyhow,
Giuseppe decides.

We rack our wine when there is very little moon to
affect it. First, Giuseppe chips away the plaster of Paris
round the bung, and puts one end of a rubber tube down
into the barrel. Sucking at the other end, he starts the wine

* *The Ancient Mediterranean* (Weidenfeld & Nicolson, London, 1969).

syphoning into buckets for transfer to another barrel or into the waiting demijohns (for most Italian wine goes 'into glass' within about six months of its first conversion from grape juice). We all have to drink a glass or two and to admire the colour and the clarity. As each demijohn, containing somewhere about eleven gallons, is filled, Gino pours in a little olive oil, to prevent any contact with the air (which it does far more effectively than any cork). Once you can flick out the oil from a flask without losing more than a spoonful or so of wine, you can claim to belong to Italy.

This use of olive oil at first made me wonder why Giuseppe collected empty tins which he puts upside down over the mouths of the demijohns—looking around the *cantina* I could see little else to explain this interest in cleanliness. Nor was a passion for cleanliness the explanation. It wasn't to keep the dust away from the oil, he explained, but to discourage mice and rats, whose passion for oil was such that they would gnaw their way through any cork. Having done so, they would either fall in the demijohn and drown, or would reach the oil by dipping their tails in it. Was he trying, I asked, to *prendermi in giro*, to pull my leg? This he denied vigorously; he had never himself seen mice getting well-oiled in this way, but everyone knew that this is what they did. And every *contadino* I have questioned on the matter has given me the same assurance.

I shall never—I hope—come to an end of this mixture of wisdom and superstition. One day before he fell ill, Gino was very anxious to spread the dung over our fields, but he could get no help from Giuseppe, who had planned to go off on his Vespa to buy some week-old chicks. (This he does in Pisa, for he thinks nothing of chicks from the Lucchesia.) Why not leave the chicks, I asked, for another day or two?

Giuseppe was shocked. This, he reminded me, was the last day of March, and the chicks would not grow up into fine birds if they were bought in April. They must be March chicks, *Marzelline*, as he called them. And although I was tempted to suggest that twenty-four hours could not make much difference to them I kept quiet; more and more I hesitate to condemn the beliefs of the countryman, so many of which are based on sound common sense and keen observation, even though they be wrapped up in what seem to be absurd superstitions.

If the wine has to be racked when the moon is waning, lest it should draw the lees up from the bottom of the cask, I had expected that our maize would be sown when the moon was waxing, so that it would be helped to grow. Gino had no views on the matter; Giuseppe was sure such a procedure would be wrong, although he could not explain why. The theory seems to be that one waits for a waxing moon to sow root vegetables and a waning one to sow plants that grow upwards. The sooner a plant destined to expand under the surface can be encouraged to get a few leaves up into the sunshine, the better it will flourish; one that is destined to grow tall in the hot sunlight needs to be discouraged from precocious growth.

But there is also a belief, widespread over Europe, that all sowing should be done under a growing moon, and I am again unable to decide how much of the advice given me by Giuseppe and Gino is based upon experience and how much is in the same category as the nonsense—also widespread in very many countries—that only an edible mushroom will not blacken a silver spoon or can easily be peeled. John Ramsbottom, in his King Penguin *Edible Fungi*, writes that the former superstition dates from the second century B.C., and that the latter is a century older. Having eaten over a score of different fungi in England, many of which would have passed neither of these tests, I have learnt that the fungi of which I must be careful are nearly always those which have so foul a taste or smell that I should not want in any circumstances to eat them, and that nobody who follows the advice given in one of the several little books on the subject is likely to come to any harm. (One of the books I possess on the subject, published as long ago as 1894 by—rather unexpectedly—the Society for Promoting Christian Knowledge, names the following among the poisonous mushrooms—Buff warty caps, dung slimy caps, sulphury mushroom, green slimy caps, wood woolly foot, bitter straw russule, acrid milk mushroom, sham mushroom, emetic russule, fiery milk mushroom, bitter boletus, satanic boletus and lurid boletus. With such names, might one not expect everybody to look for advice?)

But I am not so sure that advice can always be followed. Differences of climate and circumstance produce so many sub-species of birds and plants and insects. May they not also change the qualities of the fungi I have been taught to look on as safe? I wrote, in *Tuscan Retreat*, of the anxiety of the Russian soldiers, in the autumn of 1941, when they saw me nibbling an ordinary field mushroom (*Psalliota campestris*) during my visit to the Russian front. They were obviously anxious not to have a dead foreigner on their hands, and I was at least as anxious not to find myself in that condition. Possibly, had I persisted, they would have concluded that the British were some kind of super-men, but weakly I threw my mushroom away—the soldiers were, for the most part, ordinary peasants who could not afford to neglect good or tasty food : was it possible that a mushroom for which one was prepared to pay high prices in England had developed some new toxic quality on the other side of Europe that caused even the poorest people to reject it?

And in my early days at San Ginese there had been the protests by Berto and his daughter, Antonietta, when they had met me with a basketful of splendidly fresh mushrooms. They were definitely poisonous, Antonietta had said, with all the assurance of her thirteen years. Nevertheless, I told her, I was going to have them in a casserole for supper. She was not as disturbed as she ought to have been by the appearance next morning of a man who ought to be dead—

the mushrooms, she explained, were poisonous only for Italians.

But Antonietta was less mistaken than I had thought. I accepted one day a few mushrooms without asking whereabouts they had been found. Had I known that they came from the edge of our copse, and not from an open field, I should have examined them with more care. Only when I had eaten most of them did I notice the yellow stains on the stems of a few Annunziata had not cooked. This was my first experience of the Yellow-Staining mushroom (*Psalliota xanthoderma*) of which the Ministry of Agriculture and Fisheries writes: 'although not fatal, it is known to cause discomfort and illness in some persons', of whom, I discovered, I was one. And yet there were so few subjects connected with agriculture on which I could speak with greater authority than Giuseppe that I dared not admit to him I had made a mistake; the subterfuges by which I hid from him and Annunziata the fact that I had poisoned myself have no place in this book.

But I find in Italy much the same contempt for the blackberry and other free fruits as I used to find in England. And yet the blackberry is surely a pleasant fruit to eat, even if its pips do get lodged between one's teeth. How much, I ask myself, is this professed contempt really due to a pathetic kind of pride, a fear that to eat so common a fruit as a blackberry, so cheap an animal as rabbit (or as a rabbit used to be) or so cheap a fish as skate (although few fish are more delicious than *raie au beurre noir*) would be to make public confession of one's poverty.

That lovable Labour M.P., David Grenfell—at one time 'father' of the House of Commons—who worked in the coal mines from the age of twelve until he was thirty-five, once told me of the bitterest memory of his childhood. His father, a miner, had long been out of work, and the children were devastatingly hungry, however much their mother sacrificed herself to give them food. There would be nothing to eat at tea-time, but every day the mother would open the door on to the street, and shake the imaginary crumbs from the tablecloth. Doubtless the neighbours knew, for they were in much the same state of penury, and yet they mustn't know! Pride, they say, comes before a fall, but not that sort of pride.

* * *

Each year, pride has a remarkable effect in this household shortly before Easter. In the ordinary way, Annunziata most certainly belongs to that category of wives who carry out their promise to obey their husbands. If I ask Giuseppe any question about the running of the house, he denies all knowledge of it—that is Annunziata's job. If a cat is sick, or he wants to give me the letters handed to him by the postman, or someone upsets a glass of water, he calls on his wife, and she comes forward without hesitation. And this is not merely because Giuseppe is a man who expects to be obeyed; even Gino, as good-natured as any man I know, orders his wife about, because that is one of the God-given reasons why wives are there—the Old Testament puts women in their place, and in this respect, despite the immense importance given to the Virgin Mary, the Catholic Church seems rather to follow the Old Testament than the New.

But the status of wives changes temporarily shortly before Easter. Gino would find that he had to spread the dung or bring in the olive prunings as best he could alone, for Maria, Annunziata and the other women in the neighbourhood were busy with their *Pulizia di Pasqua*, their Easter Cleaning. Before the priest comes to bless each house everything has to be cleaned, washed, polished, with a thoroughness that would astonish most women in England. In early spring there is a great deal to be done out-of-doors, and I suggest to Annunziata that the priest is unlikely to notice every speck of dust on the picture frames or every dirty mark on the whitewashed walls, but my satanic temptations are

rejected. I should console myself with the reflection that, as a widower, unused to looking for dirt under the carpets or dust on the shelves, I should probably live in squalor were it not for the village priest and his blessing of the house. I am expected to slip an envelope with a thousand lire or two into a basket carried by one of the acolytes, but I reckon the priest's visit is very cheap at the price.

I have the advantage over all my neighbours in that my house is first on his long round. The bells of San Ginese ring out when he is leaving the church with the holy water and the two small acolytes. Until recently, I have enjoyed the sight of this small, white procession coming down the path between the cypresses and the olive orchard. But we all get old and many of us get fat; our priest is round, red-faced, and he tells me all about the trouble with his liver. So now he comes in one of Fiat's smallest cars. This gives him even more time to sit over a cup of coffee and to talk about the state of the world. For him, a discussion with a foreigner, and especially a foreigner who once was a British Member of Parliament, is an event, an occasion. What, he asks, do I think about the political situation? If I told him, he would be dismayed for he expects the Church to remain stationary in a country which is changing faster than almost any other in Europe. (Pope John XXIII, who seemed to so many millions of people outside Italy to be a great and lovable old man, seemed to many Italians to be a dangerous revolutionary.) So, as soon as I can, I bring up the subject of the olives, about which he will talk happily and at length. The olive oil of Lucca, he frequently reminds me, is known to be the best olive oil in the world.

I don't know whether he takes any credit for this, but I have noticed that, on the eve of Palm Sunday, Gino used to clip olive twigs off many of the trees. This, he explained, was not some mild form of pruning; he collected them so that they could be taken to church next day to be blessed. This is said to be good not only for the trees; the twigs are hung up in the house and the outbuildings to give protection and prosperity. This seems to me much more picturesque than the distribution of a strip of dried palm leaf, knotted in the form of a cross, that used to be handed to me on Palm Sunday when I was a small boy in Bournemouth. And I imagine that palm trees were not much more common in Jerusalem two thousand years ago than they are today, and that most of the branches placed on the road along which Jesus rode his donkey into that city came not from palms, but from olives. Olives are mentioned so often in the Bible from that evening when the dove flew back to Noah in the Ark, 'and, lo, in her mouth was an olive leaf pluckt off, so Noah knew that the waters were abated from off the earth'.

Our priest does not, I think, resent the fact that I am not a Catholic. He lacks that devastating fervour that impels people to force their beliefs upon other people, even, if necessary, with the help of terror and torture. Basically, he is a humble man, and therefore a tolerant one. He would be very distressed if he knew that, when he asperges the house with holy water, he reminds me of a day, some fifteen years ago, when I saw the performance of miracles, and was sickened by the fanaticism that causes them and can be caused by them in the name of God—in this case, the Hindu God, Subramaniam. On that occasion, too, I was asperged with holy water which contained, my guide assured me, extracts from every orifice of a cow—holy water, nevertheless, to the thousands of gaily-dressed Hindus who were attending the Thaipusam festival.

This was on the island of Penang. I have since attended these festivals also in Kuala Lumpur and Singapore, but the memory that is etched most clearly on my mind is of the steep steps up the hill-side to the last temple in Penang to be visited by the pilgrims and penitents. They carried 'kavadis', gaily-coloured but very heavy contraptions that normally rest on the shoulder. But on this day most of them rested on dozens of little spears that stuck into the penitents' sides.

One man I saw had row upon row of safety pins fastened into his back, but the police had put a stop to the man who used to drag his family along in a cart by hooks fixed into his shoulder muscles. Many of the pilgrims had skewers which stuck horizontally through both cheeks or vertically through the outstretched tongue. Some of these dazed pilgrims with spears in their sides kept up a kind of shuffling dance. Their relations and friends screamed encouragement as they staggered up the steep steps to the temple where their pilgrimage ended, and where the skewers and spears were finally removed. A few minutes later, they came out again into the sun, each triumphantly carrying a coconut shell containing some of the coconut milk with which they had washed the idol's feet.

And the miracles? During the whole day I saw not one drop of blood, except on the heads of infants and small children whose heads were being shaved by half a dozen barbers in a long shed to commemorate their first attendance at the festival. Miles back along the route, I had noticed an old woman with a skewer through her grotesquely swollen tongue. Her hair was already bedraggled with sweat, and she looked wild and half-witted; Goya would at once have picked her out, even in this amazing crowd. Late in the afternoon I saw her again, being helped up the last few steps by her children. There should be some attempt to maintain dignity in old age, and I was deeply shocked by the sight of this poor old woman.

Half an hour later, I came across her once more. The skewer through her tongue had been removed. She was seated on a stone under a tree, and was combing her hair. She looked like a dull and respectable grandmother on a day excursion. And her tongue must have resumed its normal size, for her lips were drawn in over her toothless gums. After at the most half an hour, none of the pilgrims I saw had the slightest sign of a scar. No blood and no scars.

Some form of hypnotism, one is told. But nevertheless a

kind of miracle. This mortification of the flesh, this contempt for pain, may be good for the immortal soul. The history of Christianity's early saints is packed with triumphs of mind over matter. Nevertheless, I prefer the village priest, with his rather simple beliefs and his understanding of human failings. I believe he would be amused, rather than censorious, if I told him of an incident that happened to me many years ago in Geneva. But I have not had the courage to test my belief.

I was walking with a colleague through a park in Geneva during a session of the League of Nations Assembly, and we were discussing the obstructive behaviour of one of the Latin American delegates, who, in common with quite a lot of other Latin Americans, had 'Jesus' as one of his names. 'I wonder,' I said, 'whether his father was called Joseph and his mother, Mary.' Hardly were the words out of my mouth when a large and very spiky chestnut fell on my bald head. Merely a coincidence? Many people would say not. Our parish priest, I suppose, would be one of them, but he would say so with amusement, rather than with reproach, in his eyes.

\* \* \*

I have already mentioned that Giuseppe is a man who expects to be obeyed—in the right uniform, he could pass anywhere as a naval captain or an army general—and that even Gino, so gentle and good-humoured, was in no doubt that the duty of a woman is to obey. Annunziata proposes; Giuseppe disposes. He never questions an order from me, if and when I give him one, but his behaviour to the others reveals his desire to dominate. He sometimes reminds me of a song that was very popular in Germany shortly after the war, when the Germans were so down and out—do you still remember?—that a damned fool of a British demolition officer could take me to a hill above the ruins of Essen and assure me, speaking as an expert, that Germany would not be a power again for well over a hundred years. '*In Meiner Badewanne*,' sang the Germans, '*bin ich der Kapitän*' (In my bath-tub, I'm the captain).

In retrospect, I realize how much my early behaviour must have disrupted some age-old traditions that Giuseppe had inherited. I felt that I could really be of some use during hay-making and the harvest. I was proud of myself when I mastered the neat twist of the fork that enabled me to throw the hay into the air in such a way that the green side of it came down uppermost. But when it came to piling it in great mounds until it was ready to be carried to the hay-loft, I broke many unwritten rules, the most important of which was that only Giuseppe or Gino could decide where these mounds were to be. At first I thought it absurd, almost to the point of rudeness, if I started a mound and Giuseppe came along and, with apologies, moved it a few feet in one direction or another. I had not then realized that he was taking into account the space that would be needed to turn the tractor when the time came to cart the hay to the barn. In my early and more ignorant days, I had occasionally piled up the hay myself in one of the smaller fields when the others were busy elsewhere. Proudly and carefully, I had patted the mounds down with the fork and pushed in the fringes with my heel, to make them firm and tidy, and quite possibly, by chance rather than judgment, I had built them in the right place. But that was unimportant compared with the fact that, unconsciously, I was undermining Giuseppe's authority. It was as though I had taken over the wheel of a ship without the captain's authorization to do so. Now I know better. I know that even Gino would not have begun to build a mound until he had consulted Giuseppe about its location. I know that, only in its very early stages, am I expected to put hay on this mound—that is, or is deemed to be, the expert's job. Mine is the much more humble job of joining the women in collecting the hay in two parallel rows down the field so that it may be within easy reach of the expert's fork.

# TUSCAN HARVEST

My task became a little more dignified when the hay was loaded on the tractor to be carried to the barn. Gino stood in the truck, piling the hay that Giuseppe and I forked up to him. I carried loads that were probably less than half those carried by Giuseppe, I could not always get the hay off the fork without Gino's intervention, and I had not the knowledge always to bring the hay to the side of the truck where he could best deal with it. He knew, also, that he was in constant danger of being impaled on the prongs of my fork. But at least I was doing a man's job, even if I did it inefficiently, whereas Maria went up and down the field dragging behind her an immense wooden rake. Gino rose higher and higher on the hay until the effort to pass more of it up to him became too much for me, and I stood by, thanking Heaven that we no longer depended on one of our cows to get this mass of hay back to the barn. We would rope the load down, so that it almost pushed Giuseppe off the driving seat and he could barely change gear without hitting himself in the stomach. For once, Gino would have the best of it—he lolled in unusual comfort on the top of the hay, with no care in the world except that of burrowing down into it when we passed under the lime trees, lest he suffer a fate similar to that of Absalom in the Bible.

When, after much shouting and grinding of gears, the tractor was brought as close as possible to the wall of the hayloft, my own task again became extremely humble. While Gino, on the tractor, forked the hay up to Maria, just inside the loft, who passed it on to Giuseppe, somewhere high up in the remote interior, I had nothing better to do than wander round the tractor collecting the hay that fell between Gino's fork and Maria's. I tried to convince myself that even this was quite a skilled job, since the chickens concluded that the whole show was staged for their benefit, and were too stupid or too greedy to realise how great was their danger of being stabbed by one of the prongs of my fork.

When the corn harvest comes, the male's assertion of superiority becomes still more pronounced. In England I had learned, many years ago, how to stook the wheat, and my stooks withstood the wind and rain as well as most people's. But here there is often an intermediate stage between stooking and building a rick. Giuseppe has to decide where the small, intermediate ricks are to be placed, and neither of the women (nor I) would venture to do more to their building than place the sheaves, facing inwards, in a large circle, so that Giuseppe has them to hand. When the rick itself has to be built, then Giuseppe comes into his own; we are his slaves.

He begins by building an ordinary stook, standing as steeply as it can be made to stand. Round and round he goes, leaning sheaves up against this central, but so flimsy, tower, until he has a circle between thirty and forty feet in diameter. On this he builds, with the grain always facing inwards and upwards, so that rain will do it little harm. There will, in any case, be too little rain for the rest of the crops, and, as far as the grain is concerned, this is just as well, for no ricks are thatched—a little loose hay spread over the top or, when serious thunderstorms threaten, a sheet of tarpaulin with a brick hanging from each corner sees us through until after weeks of waiting, the threshing machine comes trundling up the drive, with its tired and thirsty team of men. So little danger is there of the wheat becoming wet enough to smoulder or sprout that I once found Giuseppe standing on a half-built rick, welcoming with loud laughter a fairly heavy storm because it would do so much good to the maize.

And for Giuseppe to laugh in the rain is quite something, for, like most Italians, he has a horror of getting wet. The Englishman is so accustomed to rain that he barely notices it—were he to stay indoors on its account he would grow pale and sickly for want of fresh air. Such Italians as have to be outside their houses in the rain make the fullest use of their self-training as trick-cyclists—they ride along, holding up their umbrellas with one hand and waving their greetings to their friends with the other. I do many things that serve to convince Giuseppe that Englishmen are mad; nothing, I imagine, does more to strengthen this conviction than my habit during my earlier years here of putting on my swimming trunks and working in the garden during a heavy shower on a hot, thundery day.

A paragraph about Italian cyclists, to supplement my comments about them in *Tuscan Retreat*. The ordinary pedal cyclist thinks nothing of riding along with an unwrapped scythe over his shoulder. I have seen one cyclist wriggling out of his jacket as he rode, and one motor-cyclist whose pillion passenger was carrying a sheet of corrugated iron. Silvano, the carpenter, brings planks of wood with him on his Vespa when he comes to make another bookshelf. A waiter riding a bicycle and carrying a tray with two cups of coffee is a common sight in Lucca. Heavy sacks on handle-bars do not seem to worry pedal cyclists, and I have several times seen a motor-cyclist with a small child in front of him, his wife on the pillion seat and a second child squeezed between its parents. (And yet no other Europeans show a greater devotion to their children than do the Italians.) But the limit of these dangerous acrobatics was reached recently when I passed a motor-cyclist whose passenger was standing on the pillion saddle, with his hands on the cyclist's shoulders —the only thing to be said in extenuation is that I, a very slow driver by Italian standards, did actually pass these two young lunatics.

G

## Chapter Three

I HAVE written little so far about Giulietta, the only child of Maria and Gino, except to comment on her quietness, her modesty and her beauty. We saw little of her, since she was away at work for much of the day, but on Sundays I drove her and my wife down to Mass, after which my wife frequently worried because her own clothes were so out of fashion. Then, when we returned from a visit to Elba in the spring of 1965, Giuseppe met us with the news that Giulietta was suffering from leukaemia.

This was known in the early weeks only by Maria, Giancarlo (Giulietta's fiancé), Giuseppe, Annunziata and ourselves. Gino believed she had some form of anaemia, from which she would certainly recover, so he still went round the farm with a cheerfulness that Maria must have found it difficult to bear. He was very reluctant to agree that the wedding, previously fixed to take place in three months' time, should be postponed, and he knew nothing of the religious discussions that went on between other members of the family.

Had the doctors said from the beginning that Giulietta must not marry, things might have been easier. Instead, they put all the responsibility on the shoulders of Giancarlo. She must have no children, they told him, and left him to decide, although to go ahead with a childless marriage was a much more difficult decision for a young Italian to reach than it would have been for a non-Catholic. His fellow-Catholics would have understood him if he had found some excuse for breaking the engagement, but had he done so the effect on Giulietta's health would have been disastrous, whether or not she had been told the real reason for the decision. In fact, he gave no sign to suggest that a breach ever entered his mind. So it was announced that the wedding would be post-poned for a few months, during which Giulietta was to be taken to several specialists and on the pilgrimage to Lourdes, in which her various aunts placed far more confidence than in the specialists. When she was temporarily better, she returned to light work in the factory. During the summer heat, she stayed with dull relatives in a dull mountain resort. When she was less well during winter, she stayed at home, with little to do beyond studying the fashion magazines my wife bought for her.

Not being a Catholic, I had little understanding of the arguments that were going on between the members of the family. (Nor, for that matter, had my wife, who was a Catholic, but of a less intense, northern-European variety.) When a chance came to me to express an opinion, I urged that, since Giancarlo wanted to marry Giulietta, the wedding should take place without delay, so that they should get what happiness they could together. But some of the aunts and uncles were arguing that it would be wicked for her to marry if she was to avoid becoming a mother. The matter went all the way up to the Archbishop, but even his approval did not silence all opposition.

Eighteen months after her illness had been diagnosed, Giulietta and Giancarlo were married. My wife was too ill to go to the wedding. Annunziata was one of the aunts who refused to attend it. When it was over, we drove up to a charming little hill town called Monte Carlo for the wedding lunch, and the obvious fact that many of Giulietta's relatives were missing was explained, not very convincingly, by the argument that Giancarlo had few uncles and aunts, and it would be impolite if these were completely outnumbered.

Giulietta and her husband drove off in their small Fiat for a week's honeymoon in Venice. It rained every day, and Venice in the rain, with the plaster peeling off the walls, looks as depressing as some Victorian suburb that has come down in the world. And the day after their return to the *podere* to set up house in part of Gino's cottage, my wife died. Giulietta lived for another two years, gentle, cheerful, beautiful and, I hope, happy. I was coward enough to be grateful that I was away in South Africa when the end came. But after her death I never heard Gino singing in the fields.

Perhaps, before I began this book, I should have realized that the life of a septuagenarian is likely to be both sad and, except for the person most concerned, uneventful. I doubt whether that realization would have deterred me; I should have gone ahead, because my own experiences in this new world of old age may possibly help some of those still on its threshold. Quite rightly—since the future is in their hands—so much attention is paid to youth that there is not much time to pay attention to the aged. But the aged now so outnumber the young that people who are not themselves old will be compelled to worry about the problems of those who are. Publishers' lists are no longer complete unless they contain one book on geriatrics, a word which few of us had even heard a decade ago.

One is born helpless and one dies helpless, but there the similarity ends, for the infant is unaware of its helplessness, whereas an old man is horribly humiliated by such matters as his loss of sexual power or the misbehaviour of his bladder muscles. (It would seem that, in the age-long process of evolution, we have managed to provide ourselves with internal machinery that works reasonably well for seven decades or so, but that has not yet been able to adapt itself to the cleverness of scientists in prolonging our expectation of life beyond the three score years and ten.) We are at least more fortunate than many other species, for I read recently that, within two weeks of their fantastic journey up the rivers to spawn, salmon become aged and almost lifeless. Their bones go soft, their scales drop off and they are attacked by fungus infections. Apparently, the change from salt to fresh water causes the brain to lose control over the pituitary gland which burns up all their fat, and the calcium in their bones dissolves. A process of degeneration that takes place over a period of between twenty and forty years in a man is completed in two weeks in a salmon. So, even when arthritis does its damnedest, we may count ourselves lucky.

\*    \*    \*

One of the consequences of trying to get one's ideas down on paper is the frequent discovery of the appalling inadequacy of words. Even so fine a poet as Siegfried Sassoon—and I suppose that poets, of all writers, are the most careful in their selection of words—wrote of 'the little world of one's own, whereby human beings contrive their fundamental felicity—the self-contrived contentment of a child making a dam in a brook, or Robinson Crusoe putting the final touches to the palisade of his fort.' 'Felicity' is the same as 'happiness', even though it reached the English language by another route, but 'the little world of one's own', as Sassoon himself goes on to say, is rather a world of contentment, which is not the same thing as felicity.

'Contentment' is a state of mind reached by many people on many occasions. I associate it most often with the process of achievement—Sassoon's child building his dam across a brook or building his sand castle on which he stands to defy the incoming tide; the old woman knitting quietly in the spring sunshine; the writer on the day when he finds the right words; the man at his carpenter's bench in the little hut at the bottom of the garden; Giuseppe's sigh of satisfaction when, with that double flick of the wrist, he spreads the last handful of seed over one of our fields. It is, I think, a mood most easily reached by people who are creating something or are cooperating with the natural forces of creation, and that is why, it seems to me, one finds contentment more often in the country than in the city.

Happiness is something altogether different, something that comes from outside 'the little world of one's own', and that seldom has much to do with one's own isolated efforts and achievements. According to *Webster's Dictionary*, being contented is 'having one's desires bounded by what one has; desiring nothing more, or nothing different'. Being happy, on the other hand, is being 'lucky, fortunate, favoured by circumstance; blessed, beatified'. The dictionary gives only as the fourth meaning of the word 'having the feeling arising from satisfaction with one's circumstances or condition'. Contentment, in other words, is normally something that comes from within; happiness is something that comes from without, and is therefore something unexpected. It comes, surely, during those brief and rare moments when one feels one is in touch with the universe, God, something indescribably larger than oneself. That is why it may come during moments of copulation when two people are brought together, each trying to give to the other, in the act of creation. (Is that why, when a man wants to curse, he is likely to use the name of the Deity or one of the four-letter words connected with sex?)

\* \* \*

I am, I repeat, one of the lucky ones. Nevertheless, my wife's death, eleven months before we expected to celebrate our golden wedding, made such a difference to my life that I am filled with a deep pity for those who are much less lucky than I, who find their loneliness emphasized by increased poverty, who have no particular work or hobby to occupy them, who cannot easily make new friends. Lonely young people can always hope for a change for the better, and may even be stimulated by loneliness to heroic efforts to bring that change about; their loneliness may be a step towards greatness. But lonely old people have nothing to look forward to except death. I used to be astonished when I read of old women who kept cats by the dozen; not so now. I should do so myself if Annunziata and Giuseppe liked them better.

As soon as N was dead, the mumbo-jumbo began, often

accompanied by shocking profiteering. Annunziata insisted that the mirrors in our bedroom must be removed or covered with black—apparently mirrors encourage vanity, and there must be no vanity in the presence of death, but what, in God's name, had vanity to do with that poor dead body? There were discussions in my presence as to whether the body would keep until our sons could arrive from England, or whether it should be put at once in its coffin. An Italian friend, Guido (God bless him!) took over all the arrangements, and did his best to defend my request that the funeral should be as simple as possible, since in her lifetime she had been one of the shyest and most retiring women I have ever met. (She had already been wondering how we could keep quiet about our forthcoming golden wedding.) My prestige probably went down when I insisted that no bells should be rung during the funeral—it may have been thought that I grudged the extra money this tolling would have cost: my reason, of course, was that those who loved her already knew of her death and I had no desire to depress those others to whom she had been no more than a foreigner who used to go to Mass with them.

Women came up from the village and busied themselves in our bedroom—should I offer them some money, I asked Guido, but he said this was part of their Christian devotion. They and their unshaven husbands kissed me on both cheeks to express their sympathy. Annunziata came to ask whether N had had any black stockings, and where she kept her underclothes, so presumably they dressed that dead, useless body in all her clothes. At least, when I went to see her during the night, she looked calm and beautiful in the light of the four immense candelabras that stood, one at each corner of her bed. I tried to feel grateful to all these people who were fussing about the place. The staff of the little post office at Capannori, who had so often had to deal with my English telegrams, realized what had happened from incoming messages, and themselves sent me a telegram of sympathy—that one gesture of spontaneous kindness dissolved the lump of resentment inside me, and I wept.

It was the small, intimate things that hurt most. She had been the last person to use that cake of soap. What was I to do with the half-emptied bottles of beauty preparations? On the table by her bedside were two things I could hardly bare to touch—her note-book in which she had so laboriously written her Italian exercises and a bundle of cooking-recipes, some half-translated into Italian. I found myself saying, time after time, that N would be so interested in the behaviour of our friends and neighbours, and then realizing that she would never know. I tended to avoid the cats, who could not understand what was happening and how their lives would be changed. I noticed that my signature had become small, with a very short line under it, instead of the rather flamboyant and cocky signature with which I generally ended my letters.

I said to Annunziata that she would have to do the flowers in the future, and she put some immense gladioli into the copper jug in the sitting-room, as N had often done. But she jammed them in by the fistful and forgot to replace them when they faded. I found a few roses that had survived the storms which had so saddened the honeymoon of Giancarlo and Giulietta, and put them in the hall; they gave me a little shock of pleasure every time I came downstairs, whereas I had so seldom noticed them when N had arranged them there.

One thing I could never have anticipated (and one thing I should never be able to tell her) was the kindness of our friends. I found myself invited out for almost every meal—so often, indeed, that I had to refuse several invitations because Annunziata was so obviously depressed when she had no cooking to distract her attention. I found myself laughing, and then checked myself with the feeling that I ought not to enjoy myself. But there was no other way of recovering, and I must recover, for the sake of other people as well as of myself. I told myself that this sort of thing happens sooner or later to everyone, and generally in much worse circumstances—often after immense suffering. N had refused to go into hospital, where she had been so miserable after the car accident which had brought us to Lucca in the first place, but she had come through the two morning visits to a clinic for X-ray and blood tests far better than we had dared to expect. I had been to the clinic the day before to explain, and she had seen the doctors as soon as she arrived, despite all the poor people who had been awaiting their turn. (I hope they realized better than I did how ill she was, and bore no resentment against this foreigner who was accorded special priority.)

The verdict had been encouraging. Probably no operation would be necessary. During the preceding nights, when neither of us could sleep, I had wondered whether these internal pains could denote cancer, and I found that she, too, had had the same worry. Well, now everything would be all right. When she got a little stronger we could go off to England, where the University College Hospital would look after her, as they had looked after me twelve years earlier. And it was in that mood of hope and confidence that, suddenly, she died. We had been lucky: she was for so short a time in pain.

Mainly to keep my spirits up, I took to turning on the radio in our bedroom—N had always hated it. I worked out various things I now could do, such as travelling, which N had for long been too weak to undertake. But, despite all the sleeping pills my friends brought me, I stayed awake enough to discover that dance music was broadcast from various European stations until about four-thirty in the morning, but that every half hour, the music stopped, while the Germans in the west slanged the Germans in the east, and vice versa. Then the dance music started again. I remembered how, until well after the beginning of the Second World War, the motto that greeted visitors to Broadcasting House had been 'Nation shall speak peace unto nation' and how, even after the arrival of Hitler in the *Reichskanzlei*, I had once written an article to prove that broadcasting was the most powerful instrument for peace mankind had yet devised—any girl with a Marlene Dietrich type of voice, I argued, singing nostalgic German love songs in Broadcasting House, would be more powerful than any Nazi making angry speeches about revenge and *Lebensraum*. How wrong can one be?

\* \* \*

There is one aspect of an old person's loneliness about which I find it difficult to write, but of which I must write if my own experiences are to be of the slightest use to other old persons who may find themselves in circumstances similar to my own. Worse than the feeling of loneliness when

I had not happened to meet any of my friends in Lucca (and I used to find excuses for walking up and down the busy little Via Beccheria in the hope of meeting some of them) was the desire for actual physical and sexual contact, for the warmth of a human body next to mine. I had never imagined that sex could so obsess one's mind, except during the years of adolescence. On visits to London, I found myself crossing the road to stare at the photographs of strip-teasers who so thickly populate Soho. Only shyness enabled me to resist the shady-looking young men in the doorways of these sleazy joints, with their promises of beautiful girls inside. I had sometimes read with amazement about respected and respectable old men who had been arrested in the Park for indecent behaviour: now I understood them, and was sometimes horrified by the thought of the risks I was prepared to run. There is sympathy—often a kind of admiration—for the young man whose sexual adventures get him into difficulties; there is seldom anything except disgust for the old man in similar circumstances. This need for sexual companionship goes a long way to explain why the widower (and, I suppose, the widow) often rushes into another marriage with what society considers indecent haste. But this haste may be indirectly a high tribute to his late wife, who gave him company and a satisfying sexual life.

In my own case, I was saved from making a fool of myself by two things—by the presence of my friends and by the desire to write. 'At the end of talks with friends, talks that have gone well,' wrote Bernard Berenson in his eighty-fourth year, 'I find that I have enjoyed them far beyond the value of what was discussed and concluded. I realize that the pleasure was largely animal, psychological, and not merely mental. It was the satisfaction of a physiological need and call of nature to chatter, and chatter seems in all animals to be more satisfactory in unison.'

I have no doubt about this animal need to chatter, and have often listened to the monkeys in the Malayan jungle

yelling their hearts out and presumably deriving much enjoyment from the process. On one occasion, near Fraser's Hill, I even stimulated them to continue; my first attempt to imitate them caused a shocked silence, but after two or three other attempts they joined in, having decided either to accept this unseen contributor or to neglect him. And I certainly agree with Berenson that the enjoyment of many discussions with friends—preferably across a table still dotted with the remains of a good meal and an empty wine bottle or two—has gone far beyond the value of our conclusions, if any. Such meals with friends have given me untold contentment and even, on one or two occasions, happiness according to my rather exclusive interpretation of that word.

As for the desire to go on writing, I again quote from Berenson's *Sunset and Twilight*. 'My present is devastated by the dreadful urge to write. . . . I know that at my age with no unusual constitution it is almost as absurd to expect capacity for the long hours of concentration required for writing as the virility that would make a woman with child. We who are normal resign ourselves easily to the last, with even pious and manly resignation, but not to the first. Man in the end expects more from mind than from body.' Being eight years younger than was Berenson when he complained of this urge to write, I am much less able to resign myself to the loss of virility, but very much more grateful for the 'dreadful urge to write'.

This urge, in fact, has become the most important part of my life. I have mentioned elsewhere that I wrote my first short story, all about cowboys and Red Indians, while I was at my preparatory school in Bournemouth (just across the road from the former home of Robert Louis Stevenson). I was immensely proud of the school magazine in which this story was reproduced, by some kind of mauve jelly process, just as I am still immensely proud if I see a copy of one of my books in a shop window—a fairly harmless form of vanity which, I suspect, is very common among authors and one which, in my case, seldom has a chance to display itself.

I sent dreadful schoolboy stories to a magazine called *The Captain*, and thus began a considerable collection of editors' rejection slips. I sent lyrics to the *Bournemouth Daily Echo*, which printed some of them because they filled up incomplete columns and cost the paper nothing. When I had been invalided out of the Army, I found a cottage for nine pounds a year at Lamorna, near Penzance, and decided to become a great writer. Before I had signed the lease, however, I had decided to marry a Belgian refugee who had arrived early in the war from Antwerp, with a suitcase containing things she would need for a fortnight. Clearly, we could not both live on air, and I had already begun to realize that I had nothing to write about. Newspaper columns had to replace bound books.

And so, on the whole, they did for more than forty years. Since 1961, I have been free again from journalistic obligations and with more to write about than I should have had in that damp little cottage at Lamorna. This will be my thirteenth book since the war (*absit omen!*) and my sixth written in this room overlooking the Pisan Hills. In his *Letter to a Young Gentleman who Proposes to Embrace the Career of Art* (which I should never have read had it not been for that excellent craftsman in the art, Lettice Cooper) Robert Louis Stevenson wrote of authorship: 'The direct return, the wages of the trade, are small, but the indirect, the wages of the life, are incalculably great. No other business offers a man his daily bread upon such joyous terms.' I count myself lucky.

\* \* \*

That aspect of second childhood which so sharpens the old man's memory for events of his extreme youth is caused, I suppose, by some kind of nostalgia. But I am surprised in my own case how often I remember my small humiliations rather than my relatively greater successes. At the age of fourteen I went to stay with a clergyman uncle near Basingstoke, and the train stopped for a while on an embankment overlooking a copse of fir trees. Our presence frightened a wood pigeon off her nest, and I could clearly see her two white eggs. This to me (for I was then planning to write a book about British birds, which, of course, I never wrote) was a memorable event, and I described it to my uncle as soon as I arrived at the rectory. But, in my enthusiasm, I told him there were four eggs. He raised his bushy eyebrows. How interesting, he agreed, since it seldom happened that a wood pigeon laid more than two eggs. He knew I was lying, and he intended me to know that he knew I was lying. But I lacked the courage to confess my small sin, and the regret is still with me, some sixty years afterwards.

A second regretful memory is also connected with a clergyman. I had been learning how to cast a fly, and had succeeded in whipping a few very small and inexperienced trout out of the Lyn, river of such happy memories. I went to stay with the rector of a village near Taunton, and he had advised me to bring a rod with me, as he had a small stream. Small it was, indeed. Nothing more than a trickle, with one or two deep pools, in which lived trout far too canny to be deceived by the March Brown or whatever fly I plumped on to the surface of their pool. Day after day I fished that damned stream, without success and with growing shame. Generally I took a gun with me since, if I could not catch a trout, I might sometimes assert my manhood by shooting a rabbit. On my last day, when a large trout rose to take a supercilious look at my fly, I quietly put down my rod and took up my gun. The fish was still near the surface, and I shot at it. Stunned, it turned on its back, and floated, belly upwards. Hurriedly I grabbed it, and went back in triumph to the rectory, where the praise I received turned to dust and ashes.

One final small confession, dating from the time when I was already a father. I went one day into the bathroom, and pressed the tube of toothpaste. The paste came out in thin, vermicelli-like coils from at least a dozen holes. Someone had obviously enjoyed the idea of converting a humdrum tube of tooth-paste into something resembling a hedgehog. One of my sons, then about seven years of age, confessed that he was the criminal and, in a moment of stupid and unreasoning anger, I clouted him so violently that he staggered right across the bathroom. (It wasn't a very large bathroom). Thereafter for months I reproached myself for punishing so roughly what had been a very minor misdeed. Quite possibly, I told myself, I had affected his whole attitude to life, his whole conception of decency and justice— psychoanalysts find far smaller reasons to explain some eccentric behaviour in later life. When he himself had reached parenthood, I one day told him how deeply I had regretted my stupid act. Had the memory of it, I asked, rankled during the years? It had not. He could remember nothing at all of an incident I still cannot forget.

\* \* \*

'Second childhood' need not necessarily mean senile decay, but it does mean that one becomes increasingly interested in age—old age and youth. Just as there is a law of averages that often causes old men to run after young girls, or thin men to marry fat women, or tall men to marry very tiny women, so there seems to be an increasing readiness in old age to recall the events of one's youth. . . . After all, youth and old age are the periods when one is most acutely conscious of one's loneliness. Youth has to face the intimidating adventure of life; old age has to face the intimidating adventure of death. Youth faces his adventure with energy and determination; old age faces his with resignation. But it seems to me natural that old people should seek some reassurance by returning to the memories of youth.

But so much that is remembered is distorted by one's imagination or is of no significance. I can remember the initials of so many of the boys who were at school with me, but I have forgotten everything else about them. I remember the names of the girls with whom I fell desperately in love, and yet their names were completely unimportant. At one period the appearance of each of them must so have obsessed my mind that I thought to recognize her in almost every girl who walked towards me down the street. That must be her! And when the girl came close, I felt ashamed that I should have so insulted the loved one as to mistake her for this ugly and ungainly female.

But what, in fact, did these loved ones look like? Kathleen Raven, with whom I used to hold hands at my kindergarten? Kathleen Musgrave, who made my holidays from boarding school so wonderful or so agonizing? Ina Eichholz, who tried to teach me German under the apple tree in that Bromberg garden? Reidunn Kaassen, the Norwegian with whom I used to sit in the gallery of the *Opéra Comique* (price 75 centimes) to hear tubby tenors and large-bosomed sopranos expressing, in Puccini's music, the love I believed I felt. And all those others who came into my life after I had reached manhood—at most, I can remember one woman's chin, another's eyes, another's hair. And if we were to meet, and to compare notes, most probably the events one of us could remember would be events the other had entirely forgotten.

It would almost seem that the incidents which were most important at the time of their occurrence are those which fade most quickly from our minds. As a foreign correspondent and as a Member of Parliament, I have met many of the people who were famous in their day. Possibly because I was so anxious to register their appearance, their opinions, their voices for the next day's newspaper, they have left a less durable impression on my mind than scores of much more humble people. Three times I interviewed Hitler, or was shouted at by him, and I cannot remember whether his eyes were blue or brown. I remember only that silly little moustache, that unattractive quiff of hair and that angry, querulous voice. Of Stalin, I remember that he was much smaller than I had expected (I suppose that he shared with other dictators the desire to be photographed from knee level, so that his appearance would be more imposing than reality), that he walked on his heels, and thus appeared rather to glide than to stride, that I wondered how a man with his record of ruthless cruelty could look so benevolent. I remember of Mussolini his habit of opening his eyes so wide that one saw the circle of white all round the pupils. Of Gandhi, I recall that his ability to answer awkward questions by speaking in parables sent me back to the New Testament to confirm my conviction that Jesus had employed a similar tactic.

John Masefield (who wrote passionate adolescent poems

to one of my aunts which disappeared mysteriously after her death) I recall as a quiet and very gentle old man, to whom I should never have attributed the tough adventures of his youth. I remember Lloyd George not only on account of our political discussions at Churt, but also on account of my wife's dismay when she discovered, to her cost, that, in his old age and in common with a lot of other old men, he had an irresistible desire to pinch women's bottoms—her dismay turned to anger when I suggested that the two resultant bruises were of no value since she had not got him to autograph them. Of Neville Chamberlain, whose Munich policy I distrusted so much that I stood for election to the House of Commons in opposition to it, my keenest recollection is an unexpectedly sympathetic one—we journalists were waiting in the lounge of the Hotel Petersberg, near Bad Godesberg, to learn whether he was going to reject the claims, amounting to abject surrender, which Hitler wanted to impose upon the Czechoslovaks, and hour after hour we could hear the Prime Minister pacing up and down above our heads, while he faced the alternatives of defiance or surrender to that evil man. Faced with such responsibility, he had all my sympathy and pity.

Dr Dollfuss was a courageous little Austrian Chancellor whom the Nazis murdered when they marched into Vienna. I recall him best in very different circumstances. I was interviewing him in the Hyde Park Hotel when the burning ash of my cigarette fell inside my waistcoat, and there was the Chancellor, hopping round in front of me and slapping me on the chest and stomach in a way that would certainly have amazed anybody who had happened to enter the room. Jan Masaryk, that other victim of dictatorship, is one of the few statesmen whom I remember with complete clarity, and with an unbounded admiration for the ribald jokes with which he maintained his own courage and that of his friends during those shocking days of the Munich crisis—the Communists are even more guilty if they drove so brave a man to suicide than if, as is more probable, they killed him by throwing him out of the window of the Czernin Palace in Prague.

George Bernard Shaw I remember less for his famous and witty postcards than for his personal kindness to young writers, such as myself. (I had hoped to get one of these postcards to help me when first I stood for Parliament; characteristically, his reply expressed the hope that the electors of Bridgwater, whose votes I so needed, would not vote for me—I was too useful a man, he added, to shut myself up in the House of Commons.) H. G. Wells, the other great stimulator of the young of my generation, I remember less for the discussions we used to have about the future of the world than for a voyage we made together from New York during the great slump in 1930—there we sat, two tubby and unromantic-looking men, in an almost empty lounge, while he begged me, almost with tears in his voice, to persuade a mutual friend to marry him. (Fortunately for both of them, she was far too intelligent to reduce her influence over him by doing so.)

I remember Malcolm MacDonald more clearly than most of the other important men with whom I have come in contact—and I rate his importance very high indeed, for no other man has done nearly as much to diminish the inevitable bitterness which accompanies the dissolution of a great empire. The leaders of the newly-independent states are unable to fulfil the promises they made before independence —bus fares must still be paid, taxes cannot be reduced, corruption in an inexperienced civil service is bound to increase, at least in the early years, and these leaders can save their jobs, and quite probably their lives, only by assuring the disillusioned masses that all the blame should still be attributed to their former white rulers. But in Asia and, later, in Africa, Malcolm MacDonald, by his own modesty and his sympathetic understanding of the difficulties these new countries had to face, robbed transition of its bitterness. He has been, at one time or another and in one country or another, Cabinet Minister, Governor-General, Governor, Commissioner-General, High Commissioner, Ambassador-Extraordinary, Special Envoy, and I know not what else. But all this is much less important than the fact that he seems to be entirely unaware of the barriers of colour and class, to the great annoyance, of course, of those to whom these barriers are dangerously important.

I treasure two recollections of Malcolm MacDonald. In 1955, I was staying with him in the Residency in Penang. The deep balcony which was his office was separated from the balcony which was the main reception room only by a thin screen, so that, however hard I tried to read the London newspapers, I could hear him dictating his despatches to the Colonial Office. They were important, but not important enough to prevent him from rushing to my side of the screen whenever the sea eagle brought some food to the nest high up in one of the Residency trees. I liked him for his convictions that the habits of this bird were as important as the political developments in Malaya.

Nearly ten years later, when hè was on his way to take over the post of Governor in Kenya, he came with the British Consul in Florence to have lunch with me at San Ginese. That was in the days when the *contadino*'s cottage was occupied by Berto, Nunzia and their daughter, Antonietta, whose charmingly precocious manners inspired several pages in *Tuscan Retreat*. She loved to serve at table—as did Giulietta after Gino had replaced Berto—and she always wanted to be told in advance all about the guests. So I explained to her that Malcolm was very important, since he would be the personal representative of the Queen in Kenya, a large country in Africa. I told her something of his work in India and South-East Asia, and possibly I exaggerated a little, in order to win a little more reflected glory for myself.

It was a hot day, and Antonietta liked to stay indoors to avoid the heat. But not on this day, when she was to see the

Queen's personal representative. She hovered around in the garden so that she would see the car as soon as it left the main road and turned into the drive. She called out excitedly when it did so. But Malcolm MacDonald let her and me down—he was in an open car, and wore an open-necked shirt and a white handkerchief with a knot at each corner to protect his head from the sun. It was not until I could show her, some months later, a newspaper photograph of Malcolm in full dress uniform, presenting his letters of credence to the President of Kenya, that Antonietta's confidence in me began to revive.

\*     \*     \*

So much is forgotten or, if remembered, is falsified by my imagination. Possibly forgetfulness is a safeguard—the less we are burdened by memories of the past, the more space there is in our minds for interest in the future. But I am often alarmed by the discovery that, the older I get, the less I can trust my memory. Too often, I remember things as they might have happened, and not as they happened in fact. I remember in detail, for example, one incident at Bad Godesberg, during the Chamberlain-Hitler meeting there in the autumn of 1938. I stood with Sir Ivone Kirkpatrick, later Permanent Under-Secretary at the Foreign Office, at the top of the three steps leading down to the bar in the Hotel Petersberg. At one end of the bar sat most of the German correspondents; at the other were most of the British. We were waiting while Mr Chamberlain went to the Hotel Dreesen, on the other bank of the Rhine, to take leave of Hitler—if the interview lasted less than a quarter of an hour, it would mean that the Prime Minister was standing firm— whatever the consequences—in his refusal to bring pressure on the Czechoslovak government to accept Hitler's terms. But if the interview were prolonged, it would mean that he was weakening in face of the Fuehrer's threats, and was surrendering both honour and Czechoslovakia to him.

It would be interesting, Kirkpatrick suggested, to join the Germans. It was, for most of them were quite frankly frightened lest Chamberlain should maintain his rejection of the Fuehrer's terms. The British correspondents, on the other hand, were almost unanimous in praying that the interview would be short—most of them knew much more about the reluctance of the Germans at that time to be dragged into another war than did Chamberlain or Sir Nevile Henderson, the Ambassador in Berlin. And some of them knew of the strength of the Czechoslovak army, and the importance of having Russia as an ally. (Perhaps they knew too little of the Commonwealth's lack of preparedness.)

As time passed by, the British became more and more uneasy, and the Germans became more and more cocky. In the end, Chamberlain gave way. He would not urge the acceptance of the German terms, but he would pass them on to the Czechs, and the fact that he was willing thus to act as Hitler's messenger made it quite clear to the ministers in Prague that they could not count on active British support if they defied the Germans. That night, I lay in my luxurious bed in the Petersberg, so convinced that war was now inevitable that I wondered whether the Germans would not act at once, and arrest those of us—of whom I was one—who were known as enemies of the Nazis. I was so uncertain of my ability to defy S.S. torturers that I lay awake, wondering whether and when I should get back to England, and was amazed next morning when the hotel manager obsequiously hoped I should have a good journey and should soon be a visitor again in his hotel.

All that, I remember vividly. But part of what I remember so vividly never occurred—Kirkpatrick was not with me in the Petersberg bar; he was down in the Hotel Dreesen, with Chamberlain, Hitler and Dr Schmidt, Hitler's interpreter. I suppose I was with someone else from the Foreign Office, but even of that I cannot be sure.

A week later came the wretched sequel, the meeting in

Munich. Three moments during that miserable affair are still so clear to me that I have no hesitation at all about them. I cannot forget the faces of the two Czechoslovak ministers when, late at night, they came out of Chamberlain's sitting-room after learning the terms that Britain, France and Italy had accepted on their behalf. Nor can I forget the jaunty way in which, next morning, the Prime Minister invited us into the same sitting-room and spread out a sheet of paper on his desk. On the sheet I could see Hitler's spiky signature. Nobody who was in that room on that morning could have doubted the sincerity of Chamberlain's conviction that this sheet of paper proved Hitler wanted peace in our time. Few of us in that hotel room, however, shared his conviction; most of us knew Germany so much better than he did.

But I also remember how, on the previous day, I had gone out to Munich airport to watch the Prime Minister's arrival. There stood a guard of honour of S.S. men, in their sinister black uniforms, their high black boots and their black helmets. Just before Chamberlain went forward to carry out the strange ceremony of reviewing the guard, he turned and said something to Cecil Syers, his private secretary. Syers hurried back to the aeroplane and reappeared a moment later carrying the famous umbrella, while the Germans tried not to laugh and I tried not to cry. I find it incredible that my imagination should have invented this incident, and yet, when I met Syers some twenty years afterwards (when he had become Sir Cecil Syers, United Kingdom High Commissioner in Ceylon) he flatly denied that it had ever occurred. Most of us know when we are lying; apparently I also lie without knowing it!

In the mood of self-doubt induced by these two non-incidents, I begin to wonder whether steam did in fact rise from Mr Rowland's head on days when we had curry at my Bournemouth preparatory school. I am certain that he liked his curry very hot, for I have never since been able to eat any curry except the Malayan variety, mollified by plenty of coconut milk and followed by that most cooling of sweets, *gula Malacca*. And, since he sat with his back to the window, we were well-placed to see any steam that rose from his bald head. But . . . well, I wonder.

In retrospect and self-doubt, I also wonder whether I was as intelligent a journalist as I myself believed at the time and as the *News Chronicle*, in its advertising campaigns, led several thousands of our readers to believe. I have no false modesty about my forecasts of political developments; on the whole, I came much closer to the truth than did most of my competitors, although, at the time, I had many letters accusing me of pessimism, whereas, if I read my broadcasts or articles now, I am amazed by the naive optimism that inspired them. I suspect, in fact, that it was for that reason that I became well known—I told people the truth, but I also found arguments for hoping that the truth was not as bad as it sounded. But I have to admit that, if I was a shrewder judge of political situations, I was a poor judge of many of the men who brought them about. (Incidentally, I still find it difficult to believe that my close friends are not, *ipso facto*, exceptionally good looking.)

I knew three of the most notorious British men of the last thirty years—Kim Philby, Donald Maclean and Guy Burgess—and I liked them all, and would have spoken up in their defence had I been asked about them. Indeed, Philby did for a time have a close link with a magazine I edited shortly before the war, *World Review*, and it must have been some time in 1953 or 1954 that somebody from some very important military intelligence service came along to ask whether I had any doubts about his patriotism or his politics. Doubts about Kim Philby, with that slow, attractive smile? Good God, no!

Guy Burgess, during the war, worked in the Foreign Office News Department, with Osbert Lancaster and other very intelligent men, and under the control of my oldest friend, Sir William Ridsdale. Normally, I saw 'Rids' each morning or, if he was busy, Osbert, who would talk informatively about the news in the Office telegrams while, at the same time, he was drawing his cartoon for the next day's *Daily Express*. If Osbert, too, was busy, or if the news had some special link with history, I would try to see Burgess, for his news sense and his knowledge of history were both considerable. Everyone knew he drank a lot, but I found him amusing and intelligent.

Donald Maclean I first met in Cairo at an Embassy dinner on a Thursday. He asked us to dine on the following Tuesday, and promised to telephone to my hotel. This he failed to do, and it was only months later that I learned that the week-end was the one during which he went so berserk that he would certainly have been turned out of the Foreign Service if the heads of it had not wanted to keep a man of such obvious ability.

When the disappearance of Burgess and Maclean hit the world's newspapers, I was on holiday in Cornwall. Someone showed me the *Daily Express*, with its hint that perhaps these two had gone off to the other side of the Iron Curtain. This was too much for me. I sacrificed my morning's surfing in order to go down to the village public telephone, and I got through to my editor. I knew both the men involved, I told him. They both drank far too much, and obviously they had gone on a binge, but they would be back at their desks in a day or two, contrite and repentant. 'For Heaven's sake,' I urged, 'don't let the *News Chronicle* make a bloody fool of itself, as the *Express* has done by suggesting that they were somehow mixed up in a Communist plot.' 'You can't trust anybody these days,' my editor said mildly to me a few days later. I agreed, but I still can't distrust more than about one per cent of my fellow-men.

*     *     *

My approach to, or arrival at, second childhood has not

brought with it a greatly increased understanding of today's children and adolescents. I am puzzled by the grubby young men I see lounging about in two very different places—in the men's lavatory under Piccadilly Circus and on the Ponte Vecchio in Florence. I do not feel particularly indignant about their use of the more notorious four-letter words, except for the fact that the words are so ugly in themselves. But I wonder about the reason for their use of them. It cannot be explained away as a belated reaction against Victorian prudishness and American do-goodism, for one finds this phenomenon in countries that have never passed through either of these phases of morality. It is more probably an indication of adolescent fear of the future—we of the older generations are, very understandably, blamed for facing the younger generation with the possible use of nerve gases and hydrogen bombs. Remembering the young men in the International Brigade whom I met in Spain during the civil war there, I may feel that many people between the two world wars ran risks and made sacrifices greater than most members of the younger generation are prepared to make today, but I remind myself how much easier it is to be idealistic when there is a fair chance that one's ideals will be fulfilled. Nevertheless, I find it alarming that so much of the healthy revolt of youth against nationalism and materialism should be taking forms which are likely to lead to angry reactions among older people who believe in the value of discipline and decent manners, and who still are important in that they hold power.

It surely is a little ridiculous and disheartening that the present protest of youth against war and materialism—a moral protest much more than a political one—should so often be expressed by the glorification of certain human functions—copulation and the emptying of the bowels being two of them—that normally take place in privacy, and have done so in most countries and at most stages of civilization. (There are exceptions; I remember very clearly how, during the visit I made to the Russian front during the war, the friendly curiosity of the Russian soldiers led them to follow me even to their incredibly filthy latrines, with no under-standing that I would greatly have preferred their discreet absence to their genial presence.) Copulation, or simulated copulation, on the stage may be fun for the couples involved and stimulating for the audience, but I doubt whether it brings us any nearer to the solution of the fantastic problems with which the soldiers and the scientists are facing us.

It may, indeed, make the solution still more difficult. V. S. Pritchett has pointed out that 'blasphemy and obscenity are energizers', and that sexual licence is probably a symptom of every revolution. But revolution is inevitably followed by reaction. (No revolutionaries were ever more contemptuous of epaulettes and gold braid and medals than were the Russians after 1917, but no uniforms, except, perhaps, in the more backward of the African republics, are today more bespattered with decorations and medals than those of the Russian generals.) I suspect that long before the adolescents who are stimulated by stage copulation have adolescent children of their own, a wave of ferocious puritanism will have swept over the world, suppressing not only free love but also free thought. To refer once again to the Russians, one recalls how the sexual and other freedoms professed in Russia during the early days of the revolution have given way to a *petit bourgeois* dislike of anything new in art or unconventional in behaviour. Quite possibly, the only freedom that will remain will be the fantastic step towards the equality of the sexes that is provided by 'the pill'.

Putting it mildly, most men and many women do not willingly limit their sexual activities to one person of the opposite sex—think of the Victorian fathers, complacently stroking their beards and talking of the sanctity of marriage, who kept mistresses on the other side of town! Think of the Moslems who have found it advisable to shut up their women in inner courts, well protected by eunuchs! Think of the gallant knights who locked their wives up in chastity belts before they rode away to fight in some Crusade in the Holy Land! With men and women working in the same factories or offices or enjoying together the freedoms of camps and beaches, the whole pretence collapses. And if the pill protects women from the tragic consequences of yielding to far greater and more frequent temptations than those to which their predecessors were subjected, it may perhaps be better for everyone except the psychiatrists and the writers of sentimental love stories. A young couple going joyously to bed together are probably less damaging to society and to themselves than are a young couple fumbling with each other in the back row of a picture palace or on the back seat of a car.

In one respect I find student anarchy very difficult to

excuse. In the old days, when places in a university depended upon the wealth of the parents, the behaviour of a student was a family affair, to be dealt with by an angry father and a weeping mother; now it has become national. The state—in other words, the taxpayer—foots the bill, and has some right to expect service in return for payment. Young men and women for whose education the taxpayer puts his hand in his pocket or his signature on a cheque in the hope that some of them may become the nation's leaders in politics, in industry, in the arts, are behaving shabbily, not nobly, when they carry out noisy demonstrations for or against some cause that has nothing to do with their own future education.

But here I find myself in difficulties. How can one claim that young people are too young to object to being killed? Before World War Two, the United States army consisted of just under 140,000; there are now three and a half million men under arms. Professor George Wald, an American Nobel Prizewinner for medicine, wrote recently that in his country 'so-called defence now absorbs sixty per cent of the national budget. . . . We are told that the United States and Russia, between them, by now have stockpiled nuclear weapons with the explosive power of 15 tons of TNT for every man, woman and child on earth. . . . We really would like to disarm, but our new Secretary of Defence has made the ingenious proposal that now is the time greatly to increase our nuclear armaments, so that we can disarm from a position of strength'.* And this growing power of militarism is, of course, found, to a lesser degree, in every country. Can we expect these students, these future leaders to carry on with their studies as though nothing were happening? We can't. Thank God, we can't!

What we could perhaps expect—if we ourselves had been more aware and active in the 1930s—would be fewer young people trying, with the help of sex, drugs and fancy dress, to opt out of a civilization in which, for good or ill, they are

* See *The Daily Telegraph Magazine*, August 22nd, 1969.

irrevocably involved. And I wonder whether we who are old and set in our ways do not attach too much importance to these non-cooperators and too little to those other young people who volunteer to work in peace corps and similar organizations in remote parts of the world. I was in Florence just after the floods in November 1966, and I remember how, hour after hour in the cold courtyard of the Palazzo Strozzi, young people of the kind whose clothes, whose long hair, and whose reluctance to wash normally discourages me, were rescuing the books of the Vieusseux Library. On each step of the staircase from the flooded basement to the ground floor stood a young man or girl passing up rectangles of stinking mud that could barely be recognised as books. A cold, wet, unromantic and monotonous job, but carried out in great humour. And I realized that they were symptoms of an astonishing and encouraging development, for they represented at least half a dozen different nations.

In the years preceding the Renaissance (with Latin as a common language among all cultured Europeans), students went easily from one university to another, from one country to another. At the beginning of the thirteenth century, to take one example, the University of Bologna had some ten thousand students, of whom more than half were foreigners. Wars that were waged before the Kaiser's war in 1914 did not cause the complete break between one belligerent and another to which we later became accustomed even in times of so-called peace, with citizens being deprived of their passports if they passed under the Iron Curtain into Russia or China, and risking imprisonment or death if they tried to pass under it in the other direction.

Today, alas, we have no common tongue, and there are few subjects that give rise to so much discord as that of an international auxiliary language to provide one—during nearly six years in which I broadcast regularly in the Home Service no talk ever brought me so many angry and insulting letters as one I gave about an auxiliary language called

Novial; most of them coming from Esperantists, whose language was much more complicated but also much older. (There was one occasion, however, when I bitterly regretted my ignorance of Esperanto. In 1949 I was making a visit to the communist countries of Eastern Europe, and the British minister in Bulgaria, Sir Paul Mason, was driving me to Plovdiv. We came to a small town called Pazardjik, and we stopped for a few minutes to look at the market. At once the car was surrounded by peasants, staring curiously at the Union Jack flying from its minute mast on its bonnet. Were we Russians, they asked, and when we said we were British, people poured out of every house, and, despite the years of hostile propaganda, crowded round us in the most friendly way. I noticed an elderly man pushing his way through the crowd with great determination; one realized that, for him, our visit was a major event. He spoke to the minister in a language neither we nor our interpreter could understand. So he changed over to his own Bulgarian to ask whether we spoke Esperanto. We had to admit that we did not, and the poor man turned unhappily away while we regretted our inability to give him his one great day of distinction among his fellow-townsmen.)

But, despite the absence of a common tongue, there is a level of sympathetic understanding between the young people of today that has no parallel in history. At what other period could there have been a popular French song (as there was a year or two ago) called *Manchester et Liverpool*? Is it not surprising that, thanks to the Beatles, these two cities thus stir the emotions of romantic young Frenchmen? I have a grandson who, coming from South Africa, spoke no languages except English and Afrikaans and had very little knowledge of European or Asian history or geography. That, however, did not deter him from setting out with no other luggage than a rucksack and a sleeping bag, to go down the Danube to the Black Sea, up through Russia to Finland and the North Cape, down through Europe to Turkey, across

Persia, Afghanistan, Pakistan and India to Nepal, down to Madras and across to Malaysia, and ending up in Australia. His ignorance of foreign tongues and of foreign history does not seem to have prevented him from making friends in every country through which he passed—he told me, for example, that he had spent a large part of one night sitting on a road (the warmest place) talking to a French fellow-hiker and a Turkish shepherd who had offered them cigarettes in return for matches. How the hell do they do it?

Although he is not a *capellone*, as the Italians call the long-haired young foreigners who swarm on the Spanish Steps in Rome or the Ponte Vecchio in Florence, my grandson reproached me for my failure to pick up the scrubbier hitch-hikers on the Florence *autostrada*. Had I not, he asked, spent most of my life writing or broadcasting about the urgent need for machinery to ensure peace? Had I not come to the conclusion that peace could not be achieved solely, or even mainly, by governments, but that there must be a complete change in the attitude of ordinary people? Was it not important that young people should see as much of the world as possible? Did I want them to be contented with the greed, the materialism, the nationalism of our time? Should there be no other ambition than that of keeping up with the Joneses until some megalomaniac pressed the button that would destroy us all? He had frequently heard me grumble about the increasing power of the advertiser, but was it not possible that the grubbiness and untidiness of the younger generation was in part, consciously or unconsciously, a revolt against the snobbish, glossy advertisements of smarter clothes, shinier hair lotions, larger cars?

I agreed, but with one minor and one major reservation. The minor one is that I can feel no respect for young Europeans or Americans who make their way to the poorer and remoter parts of Asia in order to beg from people whose tradition of hospitality goes with such poverty as these white beggars have never known. The major reservation is that I find no merit in being dirty. It may be true that the early saints found dirt an effective way of demonstrating their contempt for materialism, but the world is in greater need of leaders with high principles than of like-minded but un-worldly saints. Nevertheless, I took my grandson's opinions to heart.

The first couple to whom I gave a lift between Pisa and Florence were as grubby as any San Francisco hippies. Through his fuzzy beard, the young man told me he was reading philosophy at Cambridge. The girl interested me more (and not only because she was quite pretty, although definitely grey about the neck). She was only nineteen; she knew no language except a very Cockney English; her mother kept a lodging house in one of the meaner London suburbs. And yet, she told me, she was on her way home from Istanbul, to which city she had hiked some six months earlier with another girl as ignorant about the countries through which they passed as she was herself. The very day on which I am writing these words, I brought home for lunch three girls, all under twenty-one, whom I had found going along the road to Pontadera, weighed down by im-mense rucksacks but determined to get to Greece. They accepted only a very light meal because a lot of food made them so hungry when very little of it was available.

I remembered how venturesome I had felt when, at the age of seventeen, I had gone to live with that German family in Bromberg, and how the head of the family had come all the way to meet me in Berlin lest the adventure should prove too great a strain on my initiative and courage. These, surely, are two qualities which the young people of today do not lack. God knows they are qualities of which the world stands in need.

# Chapter Four

I MENTION, later in this chapter, the shortage of wild life anywhere near Lucca. This shortage, however, does not apply to reptiles and insects. Our bedroom windows are covered with gauze, and the soft, warm evenings, when one would like to sit outside, admiring the sunset or the stars, lose much of their romance if one's guests spend their time dabbing insect repellent on their faces and arms or crouching over coils of a kind of green clay that smoulder in saucers at their feet. (These coils, which we used occasionally in Singapore, where spraying by the municipality had virtually annihilated the mosquitoes, used to be made by the 'Pure Blood Company' of Hongkong; here in Italy dozens of companies with less surprising names are now cashing in on the presence of mosquitoes even in the cities, where they ought not to be.)

There are other creatures that lessen one's enjoyment— hornets and giant wasps and small scorpions with an elegant appearance and a painful sting, not much worse, in the case of the Italian scorpion, than the sting of a wasp. And there are snakes, quite a lot of them, but in all Italy only one variety of viper that is really dangerous. I therefore reproach my visitors for their fear to walk through the copse in summer—I can afford to do so, because my own fear of snakes is rather less than my fear of spiders or cockroaches. In the snake temple on Penang Island, I once allowed one of the monks to drape cobras and other serpents all round my body to please a Mexican girl with a camera—she was so attractive that any male would have run risks to win her approval, and I reckoned that the temple made too much money out of tourists to put any one of them in real danger. I was even fascinated by the snakes and by the smooth dryness of their scales. But I admit that I am happier when the rustle of dry leaves in the undergrowth is made by a lizard than by a snake, even though I am not consciously influenced by the account in *Genesis* of the serpent's responsibility for the fall of Adam and Eve.

The lizards that creep out of cracks to sun themselves on every wall are immensely attractive, and seem to be so much tamer than the other reptiles. I have watched a young friend in Cape Town catch a chameleon and hold it near a fly; whatever the chameleon felt about its captor, it never failed to put hunger before fear—it would suddenly shoot out its long tongue to catch the fly. But I suspect that, in the case of the lizards in my garden, I can approach them partly because they trust in their camouflage—if they remain quite still, great, blundering man may not notice them—and partly because great blundering man creates in them a kind of trance induced by fear, a state of catalepsy.

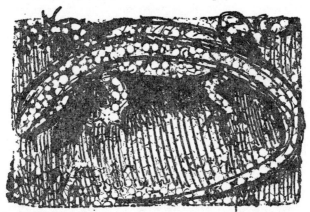

And whenever I write that word 'catalepsy' (which does not happen very often), I am reminded of the small dragon I was once lucky enough to meet near the old reservoir in the jungle a few miles from Kuala Lumpur. It was a place few people visited, and still fewer followed the rough path by the side of one of its tributary streams. If one walked quietly and inconspicuously along it, one might occasionally see a troop of monkeys, leaping thirty foot or so from tree to tree; a pair of flying squirrels gliding under the high canopy; a rhinoceros hornbill, flapping noisily and clumsily among the branches a hundred and fifty feet overhead. The emphasis must be on 'occasionally', for the chances were we would see nothing moving at all, except perhaps a leech standing on its tail on a grass stem, swaying to and fro, stimulated by the exciting smell of a human being. But just when a series of blank days made me wonder whether I should not be happier at the club, with someone to talk to and something to drink, my patience would be rewarded. Never better than on the day when I saw my dragon.

An animal about eighteen inches long leapt out of a bush on my right and ran across the path to the stream, here neatly canalized in concrete. It paused on the brink until some slight movement of mine caused it to jump into the shallow water and to run upstream along the concrete bed. It did so with a clumsiness which revealed that water was not its natural element, and I had no difficulty in catching up with it. Whereupon it abandoned all hope of escape, and waited for the end. It would even have drowned itself, for the water came a little above its head, unless I had pulled it out of the stream with the crook of my walking stick, and placed it on the bank of the stream.

And there we stood, each examining the other with amazement and fear—fear on my side, despite my enormous bulk, because this small dragon was quite unlike any creature I had ever seen, and the unknown is nearly always frightening. The bumps above its eyes gave its face a toad-like appearance. Its body was covered with rough, brownish skin, as loose as the skin on the hands of very old people. I had seen scores of tree lizards, all of which had long, tapering tails; my dragon's tail was quite distinct from its body and was marked with alternating circles of brown and white, each about an inch wide. Along its spine, from the top of its head to the beginning of its tail, there ran a ridge of bristles, about the length of the bristles on a toothbrush. Its front legs were like those of a terribly skinny human being—they made me think of Chinese emaciated by years of starvation and opium-smoking. And, under its chin, were three most improbable blobs, one bright red, one bright green and one bright purple, the purpose of which, I suppose, was to create fear.

Could the creature bite? Were its bristles poisonous, like the fins of so many fish? Could it spit venom like a snake? Cautiously, with my stick, I tested the stiffness of its bristles, and it opened its jaws, and hissed at me.

The inside of its mouth was a delicate pink, and it had no teeth. My fear was suddenly replaced by a kind of affection. The coloured blobs, the bristles, the hissing were all so much bluff. To my dragon, I must appear as large, as terrifying, as omnipotent as God. Does God, I wondered, feel a similar affectionate pity for the boastful claims and posturings of man, a pity somehow mixed with admiration for his pathetic gestures of defiance (inspired, after all, by the Creator himself)?

Having decided that my dragon was harmless, I thought of taking it home with me in the hope of taming it. It might be very rare, in which case the Nature Society would treat me with respect and gratitude. It would in any case appear very rare to my friends, most of whom visited the jungle much less often than did I. But then I became ashamed of this silly passion for possession. If this animal was so terrified of me even in its natural surroundings, what would happen to it if I were to carry it home in my handkerchief, and to put it in a cage to be gaped at by my friends? I had trespassed on its territory, not it on mine, and I had so frightened it that it was in a state of catalepsy—when I made a sudden movement, it made no corresponding movement to escape. It was literally paralysed with fear, of which I was the cause. I walked away out of sight, and came back only after ten minutes or so—it was still there, unable even to open its mouth and to hiss at me.

This complete surrender filled me with humility. I wondered whether the appearance of some jungle animal much larger than I would induce in me a similar paralysis. I suspect that I was the first human being the dragon had seen; at least in this case, the fear was caused by man's immense size, and not, as is so often the case, by man's shocking and thoughtless cruelty. At least in this case, the blame was not mine.

From my description of it the experts identified the creature as one of the rarer agamid lizards. To me, it remains a dragon. A small and helpless dragon, but, nevertheless, one able to remind me that, by driving Adam out of the Garden of Eden, the angel with the flaming sword had condemned his sons even in the eyes of the other creatures that dwelt therein.

*　*　*

One cannot claim that man has done much to rehabilitate himself in their eyes. This is not the place in which to list all the creatures that have become almost or entirely extinct as the result of human stupidity, cupidity or downright cruelty —a few of them are the passenger pigeons and the bison in North America; the dodo in Mauritius and the great auk in Northern waters; the leathery turtle and the orang-utan (both now to some extent protected) in South East Asia; several species of whale in the Antarctic. Almost as bad as the big game hunters have been the scientists collecting dead bodies for their museums or live creatures for their zoos— their rivalry has often made them ruthless.

Is it only my perennial optimism that leads me to detect signs of a change? Dark-skinned ministers in darkest Africa have been unexpectedly quick to realize that live animals in game reserves are far more likely to attract tourists than dead animals in museums. Even in the more advanced countries, the World Wildlife Fund and other organizations are stimulating us to doubt whether man's own interests are being furthered by the clubbing of baby seals, the shooting of polar bears from aircraft, the killing of karakul lambs at birth, the defilement of rivers and seas, the indiscriminate use of poisons and insecticides, the imprisonment of calves and hens in boxes barely larger than themselves.

* * *

There is very much less cruelty to animals in Italy than there used to be, when angry English spinsters would berate bewildered carters who were merely beating their bony horses, but I wonder why there was so much cruelty in the past. Civilization spread along the coasts of the Mediterranean from the East, and Dr Michael Grant* has pointed out that the early Egyptians treated animals with a care amounting to reverence. There were many animal-headed gods, and 'in later times men were called upon to say, as life ended, "I have not done evil to men; I have not ill-treated animals".'

Few Italians could have made the second claim at the beginning of this century; now things have changed. Thanks mainly to British initiative, for example, there is at last a growing protest against the indiscriminate massacre of birds —there is not much other wild life to be massacred, despite the wild nature of so much of the country; there are few quadrupeds larger than a hedgehog, except in the remoter mountains, where there are still bears, wild boars and wolves. I have already mentioned the laws that allow the million and a quarter holders of gun licences to shoot anywhere on private property except over growing crops or within a hundred metres of a house. This sounds much more democratic than the organized shoots for the wealthy on large English estates or over wide Scottish moors. And so, indeed, it is, but it is much more disastrous for wild life. The Italian

* Op. cit.

with a gun shoots at every bird he sees; the landowner, in his own interest, wants to preserve the local ecology. Some birds may damage his crops—in my own small way, I resent the immense appetite for wheat shown by the sparrows that nest under the tiles of my roof—but other birds keep noxious insects under control. And the man who loves his land loves it for its sounds as well as for its visual beauty—to him, a copse or a field is incomplete without its bird song.

The first Italian society for the protection of animals was founded in Turin in 1871 by none other than Garibaldi, but the establishment of a state organization for this purpose, ENPA, was due above all to a pugnacious English humanitarian in old-fashioned knickerbockers, Leonard Hawksley, who could often be seen in Rome half a century ago, upbraiding some carter or cab-driver for maltreating his horse. In one of the thirty-one assaults that followed his protests Hawksley lost an eye, and eight attempts were made to murder him. But he is now vindicated; in 1969, mainly owing to the initiative of the Anglo-Italian Society for the Protection of Animals and the British Institute in Florence, delegates came together for the first time from every Italian organization interested in preserving the natural beauties of the countryside to discuss, at Bagni di Lucca, what they could do to prevent the further destruction of that element of beauty provided by birds and animals. They affirmed that the haphazard destruction of wild life was creating a danger comparable with the abominable contamination of the rivers and the erection of hideous bungalows along the Mediterranean shores. To their lasting credit, they were six months or so in advance of the sudden world-awakening to the importance of human environment.

A National Committee for the Defence of the Hunter (a contradiction in terms?) has counter-attacked with a rather illogical argument. It rightly deplores the fact that so many birds die because the insects on which they would normally live are destroyed by insecticides. This might be the prelude to an admission that fewer birds should therefore be shot. Not so. On the contrary, the Committee argues that, since only one in three dead birds in Italy has died from gun-shot wounds, the guns should be allowed to bang away as busily as ever. The fact that the total bird population is smaller does not suggest to these sportsmen that they should shoot at fewer of the birds that remain.

My own greatest activity since I bought the villa was to make a path through my copse, so that I could the more easily do my stint of bird-watching. That was before I realized that the principal users of the path would be the men with guns. Among the beds and chairs and cupboards that Giuseppe brought with him, piled high on a lorry, had been a gun, but, knowing my eccentricities, he never makes use of it when I am at home, although the behaviour of our few birds makes me wonder what happens when I am away—within a few days of my return they seem to me to lose much of their timidity. In that, they remind me of the egrets in Nanking.

After the war, I had a very bad breakdown, and was sent by my paper on a long voyage of recovery. In the course of it my wife and I went to stay with the British Ambassador to China, Sir Ralph Stevenson, and his lovely wife, who were living in one of the few houses in Nanking that had trees in the garden. The first thing I noticed as we entered the front door was a gun, lying on the table where, in the old days, visitors would have left their visiting cards. The Ambassador noticed my surprise at this unusual way of welcoming his guests, and explained that the egrets, roosting by hundreds in the trees, were so much messier and bigger than any starlings that members of his staff with time hanging heavily on their hands were encouraged to take the gun and to shoot a few of them. But he knew I had suffered from this nervous breakdown, and the order went out that no shooting must take place except in my absence. For a few days the birds were bewildered by these blessed intervals of silence, and probably the noise and danger were all the greater when I was out of the way. But it appeared that, after a few days, they understood—when they saw my wife and me driving away from the Embassy, they, too, went away; as soon as we returned, they came back. That, at least, was the Embassy story, and since it is the only occasion on which I have been able to compare myself with St Francis, it is a story I am only too anxious to believe.

So poor Giuseppe's gun remains in its cupboard for all the days of the year except one, and that is a day on which I am even more anxious to use it than he is—perhaps because he has to clean it when we have finished with it. In the winter, I buy a dozen or so special cartridges and, on a cold December morning, when all the caterpillars will be at home, we fire poison cartridges into the nest of the *processionarie*. Despite my growing disinclination to take life, even of humble insects, I enjoy my campaign against these caterpillars, partly, I suppose, because some instinct still makes me pleased to hold the butt of a gun against my shoulder, but mainly because these *processionarie* show an intensity of purpose, almost an intelligence, which I find alarming, and because they eat the young buds, and thereby destroy, the stone pines which, being so closely associated with the Mediterranean, are among my favourite trees. Their determination to continue their species is as alarming as that of the wide columns of ants one meets, marching so purposefully in tropical jungles. The least of my reasons for destroying them is that I am liable to a fine if I fail to do so.

If I do not kill them off in the winter, on some warm morning in spring I find a string of caterpillars, head to tail, crossing the courtyard on the way to some secret hiding place where they will become chrysalises and, in time, the butterflies that return to the stone pines to lay their eggs in September. The longest column I have seen measured just under thirty feet. I set out to destroy them with a spade, with insecticides, with any weapon that comes to hand, and their green blood is all over the place—Giuseppe once got a drop of it in his eye, and was in pain for nearly a week. But some always survive, and I am amazed by the way in which, within at most two or three minutes, they have selected another leader, and are forming a fresh column, head to tail, head to tail.

How do they elect their leader when they start on their pilgrimage down the tree trunk? By what process do they choose another one in the midst of the chaos I have created? I am told that if you start this leader going round the edge of a bucket or a basin, it will lead its followers round and round for a long time. Nor does the leader need to be an outstanding individual, a Napoleon, a Churchill, a Mussolini among caterpillars, for if you can so arrange things that it finds itself with its head up against the tail of the last member of its column, it will plod along unsuspectingly in the circle thus produced.

Each year, I plan to mark the leader with a spot of white paint to see whether, when the circle does finally break, it will be the one to break it. But the *processionarie* set out on their pilgrimage just at the busiest time of year, and I have not yet found the courage to waste time so obviously when everyone else is so busy. I have made only one attempt to join in the sowing of maize—I found it impossible to walk, step by slow step, along a very narrow furrow, dropping a seed every fifteen inches or so; I repeatedly lost my balance and released seed by the handful, with humiliating results when the crop came up. But there are other urgent activities in which I could and should take part, and the excuse that I wanted to watch the *processionarie* would be far less acceptable than that I felt the urge to get ahead with my writing. For writing is something so far outside the experience of Giuseppe, Gino and Berto that it is treated with deference and respect.

I am, of course, flattered that it should be so—any connection with the arts carries with it a prestige in Italy that is in striking contrast with the contempt it often carries in England. As a writer, I am generally addressed as '*Dottore*', although I have never been to a university, or '*Professore*', although I have never been a teacher except, for six months or so, in a language school in Berlin shortly before the First World War. But this flattery does not lead me to forget that I produce only words, which are inessential, whereas Giuseppe and, until recently Gino produce food, which is not. Had I got my priorities wrong, I should have learnt better after Gino fell ill. (His distrust and fear of doctors dates, I think, from the one occasion when he was given an anaesthetic; he felt afterwards that he was diminished, was less of a man because he had come so completely under their control. As he explained, he might have given birth to twins and have known nothing about it.) With Gino lying in bed, I soon came to realize how nearly irreplaceable he was. Our whole routine was upset, and it reminded me of some advice received when I was a very young foreign correspondent in Switzerland from an old and very experienced one, Sir Percival Phillips. 'When you go on leave, and have to appoint someone to do your job while you're away,' he said, 'appoint the biggest fool you know, and pray he will make almost every possible mistake. Then, when you come back again, your editor in London will be glad that he has a regular correspondent who is so reliable, so energetic, so active, so intelligent.' (I followed this advice, my substitute sent a story of an avalanche disaster at Davos by mail instead of by telegraph, and I still have the telegram in which Lord Northcliffe, then owner of *The Times*, replied to my explanation. 'A very bad beginning of your work for *The Times*. It never can happen again.' It didn't, for thereafter I chose more experienced substitutes.)

Gino had never been well since the death of his daughter, Giulietta, but he collapsed with fever while I was away in Geneva. I arrived home at five in the morning, and did not want to disturb anybody at that hour. The two blackbirds that had survived the shooting season were competing with the nightingales (which, incidentally, sing all day in my copse). Everything was fresh and the scent of the roses was delicious after my night journey. I walked down the grass path between the small fields of wheat and oats. It was only then that I noticed the high weeds growing up under the vines where, shortly before my departure, Gino had turned over the earth, pushing with his bare foot on the shoulder of his long spade—neither he nor Giuseppe would ever use the spade I brought back from England; it digs too deep for their liking.

The weeds showed that there had been welcome rain during my absence in Switzerland. But they ought not to be there at all. 'Another task there is,' wrote Vergil two thousand years ago, 'the dressing of the vines, that is never finished;* for year by year three times, four times, you should loosen the soil. You cannot turn and break the clods with your hoe too often.' I went on down the path to the field of maize, and here, also, there were far too many weeds. And there was no sign of blue copper sulphate on the leaves of the vines, that should already have had their second spraying. My joy at coming home was replaced by a feeling of disquiet.

I sat for a while on the bench in front of the villa until I heard Maria opening the door of the cowshed. Gino, she told me, had been ill since the day of my departure. Every evening he had a temperature, and the doctor had diagnosed bronchitis and pleurisy and had sent him to hospital. Each time I went to see him there, I found he had his eyes fixed on the entrance to the ward, for he was desperately homesick. He hoped for company, but Maria was too busy in the *podere* to go often to Lucca. She and he both seemed less worried about his health than about its effect on the farm. And Giuseppe, who had come to me in the first place to escape

* *The Georgics.* Translation by Cecil Day Lewis (Oxford University Press, London, 1966).

from the drudgery of life as a *contadino*, became so busy doing a *contadino*'s work again that for weeks I scarcely saw him. On most mornings I would hear him driving off with the tractor before I got up, and Annunziata hurried through the housework in order to become again what she had always been until she came to us—a strong and hefty peasant.

\*     \*     \*

One has so many sad reminders of the ability of man to destroy the beauty of the scenery around him. For example, despite so strong a popular desire to be in or on or near the sea that one might think men were trying to reverse the whole trend of evolution, one finds very few indications of a determination to stop treating the rivers and the oceans as cess-pools. (The ambition of the sons and daughters of the

Swiss with whom I used to swim far out into the clear waters
of the Lake of Geneva, when I lived there fifty years ago, is
to save up enough money to build, for their own sons and
daughters, small, chlorinated swimming pools, in which they
can swim around like goldfish in a bowl. This is called
progress.) The Mediterranean, most beloved of all seas,
has more muck washed up on its beaches than any other
sea I know, and it lacks the God-given help of high and
vigorous tides to wash it away again to somebody else's
beach.

### Dialogue by the Sea

'Isn't this a lovely beach? I came here as a child.'
'Be careful! There's a beastly lump of tar.'
'We never put on swimming suits—it used to be so wild.'
'What a shame they built that beastly bar!'
'Let's walk along the beach a bit—that band makes
   such a noise.
Besides, I'd like to lie upon the sand,
Remembering the plans we made when we were only
   boys.
Oh damn! that broken bottle's cut my hand.
No! No! It's only just a scratch. But, still, I think
   we'll go.
This isn't quite the place I used to know.'

\*     \*     \*

And, of course, it's not only the beaches. Invariably, the
thrill of pleasure when I hear a mountain stream rushing
through an Italian village is followed by anger and disgust
when I find it cluttered up with old tins and buckets, bits of
broken beds or bicycles, disused boots and anything else that
nobody wants. There is a footpath from my farm up the
hill to the village of San Ginese which begins pleasantly
enough, flanked by my cypresses and olives. But I seldom

use it; its approach to the village is made hideous and stinking by the garbage thrown out of their windows by nice people, preoccupied by the desire to keep the interiors of their own houses clean and neat, come what may outside.

But there is another side to all this. In Italy, more than in any other country I know, mankind has also added to the beauty of his surroundings. I have been in several parts of the world which appeared to be untouched by man—the rain forests of West Africa, for example, the great jungle-covered mountains of Malaya and Burma, the deserts of Arabia and the Sahara, the scrub that covers so much of east and central Africa. A Native Affairs officer in Malaya once thrilled me by taking me in a motor canoe up a river still so little known as to be marked on the map only by dots—himself, he knew so much about the Unknown that he spent much of the day reading a book. And—perhaps most impressive of all—I have sometimes set out on skis after fresh snow has hidden every track made by human beings.

Such areas leave a deep impression and I have been specially fortunate in my encounters with them. But I find that scenery is above all beautiful when it reveals the co-operation between Nature and man. No wild forest is as satisfying as a copse flanked by a newly-ploughed field; no endless and empty sea so beautiful as a sea across which boats with coloured sails are coming home to some small harbour, with lobster pots on the quay and nets hanging up to dry. There is a lot to be said for the English village, with its church, its inn, its manor house and its thatched cottages. But there is even more, I think, to be said for the much older hill towns of Tuscany, each with its great walls, its castle, its cathedral and its narrow streets. How much less interesting the countryside would be if, long ago, men had not planted that row of cypresses, terraced that hill-side for their vines and olives, built that bridge so that the remote farm could become part of the community, and the community could become part of civilization. The views that one sees through arches and doorways in some naive but inspired Renaissance painting of the Holy Family are the views one sees in Tuscany and Umbria today. Nowhere else are there so many reminders of the long cooperation between man and the soil that provides him with his food.

And a cooperation that basically does not change. We no longer believe, as Vergil did, that a new swarm of bees can be created by beating a calf to death and leaving its body in a narrow cell until insects appear, 'limbless at first, but soon they fidget, their wings vibrate, and more, more they sip, they drink the delicate air. At last they come pouring out, like a shower from summer clouds, or thick and fast as arrows when Parthian archers, their bowstrings throbbing, advance to battle.' (Throughout Egypt, Vergil declared, bees could be produced in this way, but the secret was first revealed to Aristaeus, son of Apollo and the nymph, Cyrene, after the gods had destroyed all his bees because he had pursued Eurydice into the fields, where she had died from the bite of a poisonous snake.)

Also, I had doubts about Vergil when I read his claim that 'olives have no use for the sickle knife', for our olives soon cease to produce any fruit at all unless they are pruned and chopped about with a ruthlessness no other tree could stand. But he rightly mentioned, as one of the peculiarities of the olives, that they flourish in 'a stubborn soil and inhospitable hills, where the clay is lean, and the fields are strewn with stones and brushwood'. In this one respect, our soil is too rich; high up on the rocky hill-sides around Lucca there are magnificent crops year after year, but we are too low and, even before he fell ill, Gino had ceased to worry much about our own two hundred olive trees. At most he sawed away the dead branches, and our nearest neighbour has recently hired an electric saw to cut down all his trees and to sell their excellent timber. Even if we had a heavy crop, it would hardly be worth our while to collect the fruit—other oils are now imported in such quantities and village women who at one time were glad enough to grub around on hands and knees in return for some of the oil after it had been crushed, now make more money in local factories or from their own knitting machines. For that reason, I am glad that the olive industry is a dying one, but I should be sorry indeed to follow my neighbour's example. I suspect that Giuseppe has it in mind to suggest that we should do so; I will not contribute towards the disappearance of so beautiful a tree, and one which I associate so intimately with Italy (although, like the fig and the vine, it came originally from Asia).

In almost every other respect—even to the use of 'ties of willow to bind the trailing vine' (where I, in my innocence had suggested that twine would be more effective)—the methods of farming recommended by Vergil are those that are in use today. He would, of course, be astonished to see Giuseppe bringing in the hay with the help of a tractor, in place of a cart drawn by two white, wide-horned oxen. But carts drawn by large Bruna-Alpina oxen are still a considerable menace to motorists who take their corners too quickly —or, rather, the motorists are a menace to the ox-carts. And Vergil would find that Maria still spreads our white beans out on the threshing floor in front of her cottage and beats them out of their dried pods with a flail precisely similar to the flail in use in his day. (With its leather hinge in the middle, it can be used for hours on end with little more drain on one's energy than a flick of the wrist.)

No piece of Vergil's advice appeals to me more than his: 'Admire a large estate, if you like, but farm a small one.' But that is because, for me, farming is only a hobby. The government has to take another view—Italy is becoming so important industrially that no power on earth could prevent the drift of young men to the factories. Since nearly one-quarter of the population is still agricultural, this drift is in many ways desirable. But that should not mean that the land goes out of cultivation. If it is not to do so, the tradition that every farmer must be as nearly as possible self-supporting must be replaced by farming on so large a scale that full-scale mechanization becomes economically possible.

Thus I happen to be witnessing and, in a very small way, to be involved in Italy's industrial revolution. Young men—enough young men to make agriculture prosperous—may remain as farmers, but only if they can depend rather upon machines than upon patient, plodding oxen of their fathers. Despite the difficulties of mechanized farming on these rocky mountain slopes, the disused land around me—and the fears aroused in me by Gino's illness that my own land will be disused—leave me in no doubt that the small-scale farming, still generally accepted when I came here less than ten years ago, is doomed. But that also involves the doom of a tradition whereby farms are divided, at each farmer's death, among more and more owners. Since I wrote *Tuscan Retreat*, I have had dozens of inquiries from people in Britain who would like to settle in Italy, and on their behalf I have visited a good many villas and cottages that were said to be for sale. Some of them have been empty for years, and one now expects to pay more for modernization and repairs than for the buildings themselves. They are empty because, although some of the owners want desperately to sell, there is always one of them—generally living in America, and nursing the idea that he might, in old age, return to the village of his birth—who refuses to sign along the dotted line. In the Province of Lucca, every farm is said to have five owners, of whom at least one is overseas. Vergil's advice was sound and sensible in a country with a small population and wooden ploughs; I fear it is much less so in a country with a population of well over fifty millions and a common market with fertile countries such as France, Belgium and Holland.

\* \* \*

Where man has added to the beauty of the countryside, he has done so by his care, his understanding of methods of

increasing the fertility of the soil. A good farmer cooperates with Nature; where, for some reason—such as the illness of Gino—he fails to do so, he lessens the beauty of the land. A townsman may not notice that failure; the local farmers do, and I am grateful to Giuseppe and Maria for their efforts to ensure that the local verdict on our failure will not be unfavourable. Recently, I tried to give Giuseppe some extra money to compensate him for some of the extra work he undertook after Gino fell ill; his refusal was definite, and it was caused, I think, much less by loyalty to me than by loyalty towards the land. He is determined that Gino's illness—and, alas, his departure—shall not make a lasting difference to our *podere*.

148

And quite possibly it won't. Certainly we shall have fewer and smaller grapes because it has not been possible to turn the earth beneath them as often as Vergil would have advised. There will be more weeds growing in next year's crops. The olives are the first trees to show neglect, and every time I pass them I recall with astonishment that, when first we settled here, I found time to take off all the suckers and to scrape away all the bark where the ants were nesting. The acacias have entirely taken over the vineyard to the west of the drive, but it was in any case badly sited and produced few grapes. And, after all, farming—our farming, at any rate —seems to consist of a series of crises. Each winter is the coldest, the mildest or the rainiest in human memory; each summer is the driest or the wettest. Gino has an unlimited number of sayings predicting this or that disaster if something does or does not happen on some particular saint's day—the British, I imagine, lost nearly all of them after they became Protestants. And yet I notice from my diary that the days on which we cut the corn or make our wine seldom vary by more than a week from one year to another. The oats and wheat are cut between June 20 and 27; we begin the *vendemmia* in the first week in October (except in 1966, when the grapes were all in the vat by the evening of September 23).

But this routine of the seasons is never dull. As soon as we have shaken down the olives, if and when there are any, on to an enormous strip of sacking, Giuseppe is busy pruning and tying the vines. The potatoes have to be planted, the fields manured and the maize sown. Before the end of May, most of the hay has to be cut, and as soon as it is stored away in the loft, Giuseppe ploughs and harrows the fields in the hope that the hot sun will kill off some of the weeds. Before the end of June, Elisio has come with his reaping machine to cut the wheat, and we have stacked it, first in stooks, as in pre-mechanized England, and then in small, temporary stacks. Early in July, we build our ricks, pending the unpredictable day when the threshing machine will come clanking up the drive, with a man on the top of it to chop off impeding branches of the alternating limes and ilexes. In the interval, before Giuseppe begins to burn sulphur in the wine casks and to oil and repair the aged wine press, a last effort will have been made to turn the earth under the vines. The maize must be cut and threshed, the potatoes must be lifted and sorted. Somehow Maria found time to look after the cows and, with Giuseppe scything, to carry home great bundles of lucerne before the summer drought turned everything brown. Giuseppe must also feed innumerable rabbits and hens. Sometimes he dries some of the figs, by the simple process of sticking them on to thorny twigs and hanging them out of the attic windows.

And, before the end of the year, the fields must be ploughed again, and sown with grass seed or winter wheat. At odd moments, we make our own vinegar—the 'factory' being a demijohn of wine that had 'turned', and that continues, year after year, to produce as much excellent wine vinegar as we give it indifferent wine to convert. We—or, more accurately, they—make our own brooms, our own brushes, our own ladders, and, of course, our own rabbit hutches.

The routine, then, is varied, and there are frequent unexpected additions to it, some pleasant and some less so. I am close enough to Pisa and Florence for many of my friends to come over for a meal during their Italian holidays. Occasionally, people arrive with a caravan, and an appeal to be allowed to park it somewhere on my land. They will be no trouble, they assure me, and they mean it, but I have no peace while they are there. They may be truthful when they say they would prefer to fry their own eggs over their camp stove, but I cannot rid myself of the thought that I am feeding in comfort and they are not. Rain, that normally I should welcome because it will do so much good to the crops, becomes a curse, because I wonder whether it is dripping through the canvas of their tent while I am lying in dry comfort in my own bed. I resent their presence either because they are running in and out of the house on their way from or to the bathroom or because they are so stoically washing in a small, enamelled basin. And the nicer they are, the more they activate my uneasy conscience.

Some other interruptions with routine are unrelievedly unpleasant. I read recently, in the official publication of the Italian Automobile Association, that in 1968 five hundred cars were stolen every day in Italy. But Lucca is very quiet and law-abiding, and my doors are seldom closed (except when it is too cold to keep them open). But one day Giuseppe came in with the news that twelve of our chickens had been stolen during the night. When I expressed astonishment that we had heard nothing, he admitted that one of his cousins had, at one period, kept himself well-supplied in this way— one had to move one's hands very quietly up the fowl until it could not open its wings and then to pop it very quickly into a sack, where it would keep silent. A few days later all the peaches on our best tree were stolen. And then came the incident of the Muscovy ducks.

Giuseppe and Gino were both very proud of the Muscovy ducks, which waddled with strange dignity about the place. The drake had two favoured wives, one of which lived in our yard and the other in Gino's. He would spend the day with us but, at about six in the evening, he would cross the lawn, follow the path under the pergola, and wait until somebody came to open the gate so that he could spend the night *chez* Gino. Once a day, they were all allowed into the garden, where they clambered awkwardly over the low box hedges in search of snails, which they swallowed, shell and all, after alarming contortions. Ridicule is generally a form of cruelty; in the case of the ducks their absurdity aroused our affections. Even Giuseppe was reluctant to kill them—when we wanted one for the table, Gino would kill it if it had lived in our area and Giuseppe would kill it if it had lived with Gino.

One morning, Giuseppe found five of our ducks dead. A few days later, two more were killed. At breakfast the following day, Giuseppe came in triumphantly with the news that he had caught the killer. Unknown to me, he had found the only weak place in the fence and had put a noose over it. Our last duck but one had been killed and eaten, but its murderer was now lying, half in and half out of the hen run, with a noose round its neck. It was, Giuseppe said, a large *cane lupo* and was very *cattivo*. Rather less enthusiastic than he, I went to see the 'wolf dog' that was 'very fierce'.

It was a fair-sized, rather scruffy, black-haired mongrel. It was '*cattivo*' all right; fear had made it so. It responded to my reassuring tones by dashing at me and tightening the noose round its neck. To Giuseppe's disgust—for he found it difficult to remember that it was the dog's nature to attack birds, even when they belonged to us—I insisted that it must be fed, but none of us dared go close enough to give it water. What were we to do about it?

Giuseppe was optimistic. When he went down to the village, he would see the policeman, who always dropped into the bar for a morning cup of coffee. The policeman would know what to do. He would find the owner. There was no need for me to worry.

I had to go over to Leghorn on business, and returned home after dark. As soon as I entered my courtyard, I heard the poor beast howling. Giuseppe was no longer exultant. The policeman had rejected the responsibility. The *maresciallo* of the *Carabinieri*, another of Italy's several police orces, had been no more helpful. We must ring up the municipal offices, he said, and ask them to send out the appropriate official. I went out with my electric torch and threw a little food in the dog's direction; it changed its howl into a furious bark as soon as it saw me.

For the first time in years, I slept or tried to sleep, with my bedroom window shut. But, even so, asleep or awake, I heard its plaintive howl. I wondered what was going on in its mind. It must by now be hungry as well as thirsty. How could it explain to itself this growing tightness round its neck? Its attitude had shown that it attributed its misfortune to men; how was any man to quieten it down enough to cut the noose? I had had enough of Italian bureaucracy to be sceptical about the speed with which official help would arrive. And, in its absence, what was to happen to the dog, with its noose tightening round its neck every time it moved?

At about four in the morning, I fell asleep. When I got up at seven, I could hear no sound from the chicken run. Had the poor beast choked itself? What was the legal situation if it had done so—Italian laws are very favourable to sportsmen with guns and dogs; this animal would undoubtedly be classed as a game dog. I was very uneasy when I went down to breakfast, and unresponsive to Giuseppe's broad smile. Why the hell, I asked myself, had he set his trap, without even asking me? What had he got to smile about?

More than I had expected. The dog had gone. The story of the trapped wolf-dog had gone round the village, and its owner must have come to our villa to release it during the night. He alone would have been able to loosen the noose without being bitten. And doubtless he had feared a claim from us for damage to our birds. I picture him, hushing his dog's yelps at the prospect of freedom, chuckling quietly to himself over his success. What he probably did not picture to himself was my own intense pleasure that he had succeeded.

* * *

I suppose that Giuseppe is sensible, rather than sentimental, about animals. He was fond of the Muscovy ducks less because they were so attractively ungainly than because, as part of the farm livestock, he had tended them since they were very small, and had come to recognize them as individuals. He looks after his rabbits with care because he is proud of them—above all of an old buck rabbit almost the size of a basset hound. Every time a calf is born, he treats it

with a gentleness that astonishes me, but that probably has
no real basis of affection. I suspect that he thinks of it in
much the same way as he thinks of his motor-cycle.

Some time ago I woke up at about two in the morning
and heard an unusual noise of voices from Gino's cottage at
the far end of the pergola. This was before he fell ill, and at
that time the idea of illness in connection with so hearty a
man never crossed my mind. When I looked out of the
window, I saw that the light was on over his front door.
On Sundays, there are often three or four cars outside his
house, for he and Maria come from large families, but surely
he could not be having a party so late at night? I felt
momentarily annoyed—he would be too tired to do much
work in the morning. And then I remembered that he seldom
finished work before eight at night on six days out of every
seven, and I returned to bed, feeling very ashamed of my
annoyance. I turned over on the other side in order to go to
sleep again.

But then I heard a whistle just outside my own villa. The
whistle was repeated. A lover trying to signal to his beloved?
But nobody could seriously be serenading Annunziata, the
only female in the house. I realized that Giuseppe must
have been at Gino's party and that Annunziata must have
locked him out. I went to my window and asked Giuseppe
what was wrong. One of the cows, he said, was calving;
Annunziata was needed immediately, but he had hoped to
arouse her without disturbing me.

By the time I had slipped some clothes on and had gone
along to the cowshed, the calf had already been born—
considerably to my relief, for I have only twice helped to
pull on the cord attached to a calf's feet to hasten its exit
from its mother's womb. Gino had already wiped the calf
down with a sack. Giuseppe put his hand in its mouth to
rid it of the slobbering foam, and it was sucking away
noisily at his fingers. Then he threw some salt in its mouth
for the same purpose. No one could have been more gentle.

Within twenty minutes of its birth, it was staggering clumsily to its feet, with both men near at hand to save it when it overbalanced and fell. Within half an hour, still propped up by Giuseppe and Gino, it was drinking at its mother's teats. The British farmer's expression for her milk container—her 'bag'—always offends me, but I was still more embarrassed when Gino talked proudly of her '*petto*', since the Italians use the same word for the breasts of a woman. '*Guardi che bel petto,*' he used to say to me, and I would think of all the young men on the stone benches outside Lucca's Palazzo Cenami, commenting lasciviously on the fine bosom of some passing girl.

A week later our second cow produced her first calf. Again, the hurrying footsteps, the buckets of hot water fetched from the kitchen, the anxiety of Gino and Maria—since it was one of her jobs to look after the cowshed and its inmates—lest there should be some mishap. Given the fact that each new calf adds to their work but not to their earnings, one might perhaps have expected them to be unenthusiastic. Not so. Not only was their professional pride involved, but they had a deep feeling about birth and growth and death that I cannot fully share. A creature is born, takes its part in the creation of other creatures, and dies—processes which I was taught not to discuss very much in polite society. But they, not I, are the realists.

Does that mean, then, that my interest in books, in pictures, in music is all no more than escapism? Escapism from what? From boredom, which the Italian writer, Moravia, once defined as 'a scantiness of reality'? But is it not just this escapism which enables man occasionally to be aware of his kinship with all living creatures, of a reality that is 'out of this world'?

Possibly because old age gives one an enhanced respect for life, my hatred of cruelty grows more intense. There are, of course, times when one must kill in self-defence and others when one kills in an unreasoning fear of something unknown or unexpected. I realize how easily this happens when I go through my copse and feel the sudden slight tension of a spider's web across my face. I slash at the web and, if I could, would kill the spider, although I am to blame, since I am interfering with her efforts to gain a livelihood.

But I feel ashamed even when I use one of those insecticide sprays to repel the ants that sometimes invade my bedroom. Within a minute they lose control over their movements, as I suppose we human beings would do if the maniac seekers after power were to use the abominable forms of destruction which the scientists have now provided for them. The ants begin to run round in confused and distressful circles; they fall on their backs, with their legs waving helplessly in the air; they die—their tiny spark of life, so similar to my own, has been destroyed by my action. Or, if not destroyed, diverted from the course that—again for want of a better word—God had planned for it. I am aware of a feeling of guilt.

This feeling of guilt, of course, can become absurd. I remember my reflections, many years ago, when I stood in my cabin somewhere in the Indian Ocean with a blunt razor in my hand. One of the minor but most persistent problems of our time, I told myself, was solved by the sea around me. I had merely to throw the blade out of the port-hole.

I pictured the small, shining rectangle of steel, twisting and turning through two thousand fathoms until at last it came to rest in the soft, deep mud at the bottom of the ocean —mud made up of the remains of millions upon millions of creatures, many of which had lived millions upon millions of years ago. What strange and prehistoric fish, with their own little dynamos providing their own little searchlights, would hold the blade for a moment in their beams? Was not this the ocean that had provided the coelacanths? Every day, as we throbbed our way across its oily surface, we could see great turmoils in the distance, with scores of large fish leaping in panic out of the water to escape from some mysterious and still larger enemy, until our own man-made leviathan came so close to them that hunter and hunted became united by a common fear.

And I began to wonder whether the ocean did, in fact, supply the solution to my problem of the razor blade. In my boyhood, I had so often caught mackerel with no better bait than a shining hook; how far would this strip of steel be allowed to sink before it attracted the attention of some huge fish? Nothing about the sport of skin diving is more fascinating than the way in which fish accept you as one of themselves. They come, with languid curiosity, to examine this new creature, this coelacanth *in excelsis*, which has developed arms and legs instead of fins. So little do they show fear—except, I suppose, in the over-hunted waters of my beloved Mediterranean—that I, for one, would never pull the harpoon trigger, for I want no part in giving the creatures of the ocean the same distrust of humans as fills almost all creatures on dry land.

True, no fish would associate this glittering rectangle of steel with two-legged invaders of their ocean. But I began to think of the agony of the fish that snapped it up. Far worse than the agony caused by a barbed hook hidden in a juicy piece of bait. The double-edged weapon would gash its inside, and each effort to disgorge it would multiply the agony. A fish feels no pain? Even if I were to believe that lie—as I have so nearly managed to do when I have been fishing—I should still have to ask myself by what right I was destroying the small vital spark that enabled my brother, the fish, to cleave through waters still illuminated by the same sun that illumines my own arch of sky.

A further thought. The fish that swallowed my razor blade would do so because it mistook it for some other fish, much smaller and more defenceless than itself. Should I not, then, be doing a good deed by throwing overboard as many old blades as I could spare? But by what right should I thus try to upset the balance of nature. Did I think I was God?

What, I wondered, would St Francis of Assisi have done if he were in my shoes? He would not, of course have had to face it since he was not, presumably, in the habit of shaving and, even if he was, he would have had no safety razors with which to do so.

In the end, I left the useless blade in my cabin on a piece of paper at the side of my wastepaper basket. By no less direct action could I convince the steward—Chinese, and therefore very thrifty—that I wanted to rid myself of this valuable strip of steel. And later, when I returned to my cabin, I found him carefully folding the paper over this small treasure. I rejoiced that I could excuse my lamentable and sentimental indecision by the reflection that, to a man whose compatriots import millions of old horseshoes for conversion into razors, I was a kindly and thoughtful benefactor.

\* \* \*

But I do not believe that mere sentimentality leads me to deplore the fact that our cows remain in their stall from the day of their birth to the day when they are taken out to go to the slaughterhouse. The best I can say for this system is that it is less of a sin against the light than is the system now so widely adopted in countries where farming is more 'scientific' than ours and where calves are given no room to move around lest they thereby reduce the amount of tasteless meat to be sold to the unselective consumer. And we have other excuses. In the less mountainous parts of Italy, one sees cattle out in the fields, but here the fields are little more than fairly wide terraces on the hillsides, and it would be difficult to peg the cows so that they did not eat all the leaves off the vines. After a very few weeks the nourishment is burnt out of the grass, and the beasts are so unused to fresh fodder that they would need it to be mixed with a lot of hay. And, in the days when we had a cow, instead of a tractor, to pull the plough or the harrow around the farm, one of us had always to be ready with a twig to wave away the horseflies, so that she did not come back to the stall with enough blood trickling down her flanks to remind one of some 'mannerist' picture of St Sebastian and his arrows.

Also I am incorrect in my statement that our cows left their stall only to be taken to the slaughterhouse. It so happens that the annual provincial cattle show takes place in our nearest village, San Leonardo in Treponzio. On the first Sunday in September it is crowded with farmers, agricultural machinery, cows, pigs and poultry. I had no idea seven years ago how good our all-purpose Bruno-Alpina cow might be when compared with others of her kind, but Berto thought well of her, and she looked well enough to me, who had never before owned a cow of any kind. If we entered her for the show, she would get an outing and Berto and Nunzia would be encouraged. They washed her, they scrubbed her with an evil-looking steel brush, they brought the local blacksmith up to the stall to give her a pedicure, they hung a red tassel between her horns, and they walked her down to the show-ground. Feeling very out of place, I walked around the exhibitors' enclosure, trying to look like a farmer. My expectations were so small that I had gone home again long before the prize-winners were announced. But one of those prize-winners was o curow.

That was away back in 1963. In the following year we won another prize, and two prizes in 1966. I began to fear that the local farmers would feel sore that a foreigner, possibly able to buy better stock than they could afford, should win prizes in their despite, but the organizers were so insistent that we have gone on giving one or more of our cows an outing each September, even though the show has now become so important that lorries bring competitors from all over the province and no more prizes come our way. It would, I suppose, be unethical to question the opinions of the judges, but I doubt whether our old Bruno-Alpina—so much more beautiful than the Friesians we now breed—

would have been noticed had her owner not been a foreigner. But the motives do not alter the facts, and few facts have surprised me more, in a life that has included more than a fair share of surprises, than that I should have been successful with my cows at a cattle show. I, whom the farmers at Washford market so embarrassed with questions about agriculture when I was bold enough to stand as one of their candidates for Parliament! I, who would still be unable to answer most of their questions!

I have developed some scepticism about judges since I was asked to be one at a beauty show in Singapore. One fellow-judge was Francis Thomas, then Minister of Communications and Works. The other judges, as far as I remember, were the Chinese wife of the Chief Minister, Lim Yew-hock, and a Malay and an Indian lady. The competitors were racially even more mixed; racial and political prejudices were not far below the surface. And just before the judging began, Francis Thomas whispered to me that he had forgotten his glasses, so that, where I could see beautiful and shapely females, he could see only large blobs of pink, blue, yellow or whatever colour each competitor was wearing. Prompted in whispers by me, he gave his opinions to the other judges with at least as much assurance as any of the judges at our September cattle show.

\*    \*    \*

Cats, in Giuseppe's view, are useless except for killing rats and mice. I find them useful in another respect, that can best be expressed in doggerel:

> When I am guilty of the sin of vanity
> My cat assures a quick return to sanity.
> Preoccupied, he passes proudly by
> With no acknowledgement that I am I.
> He does not hear, he does not even see,
> A man so insignificant as me.

In order that they may kill rats and mice, Giuseppe reminds me, they should be hungry, and I am betraying the interests of the *podere* if I give them food. I understand his argument—which he expresses only by the most tactful hints—but I do not accept it. When I lunch out of doors, at the stone table under the wistaria, I lack the nerve to take all the food for myself and to give none to the cat, sitting patiently by my chair and miming a 'miaou' it knows it must not utter. Giuseppe's careful argument is naturally reinforced by the fact that, after more than eight years, he and Annunziata are still reluctant to eat the same sort of food as I do; in that respect, they recall middle-class life in the days of Queen Victoria, when the servants in the basement were expected to eat food of a quality inferior to that served in the dining-room.

If I have one of our chickens, Giuseppe and Annunziata will eat little of it except such unattractive oddments as its neck. If I leave on the dish pieces that I would greedily have eaten, I find them days later in the ice-box. Doubtless, in some cases they prefer the food to which they have always been accustomed to the food for which N used so laboriously to translate recipes from her French cookery books. But, even so, they know the price of the raw materials—for Giuseppe buys most of them down in the village—and of the olive oil or the butter that Annunziata has used in the cooking, and they must resent the fact that the cat (for now there is only one) should be given some of the finished product.

Shortly after we first came to the villa, I one day saw Giuseppe throwing stones at one of the cats which, mis-guidedly, was using his onion bed as an earth closet. I doubt if he would do so now: he has been amused by too many generations of kittens to be hostile to them when they grow up. Annunziata, on the other hand, still dislikes them, as one can see by the care with which they keep well away from her, although they depend on her for most of their food. Since N's death I have been away so much that the cat population is now reduced to Rufus, a rather wild tom cat with so many scars received during his love adventures that he reminds me of Hank Wales, an American newspaper correspondent who used to boast that he had a scar for every peace conference he had attended between the two world wars.

Nonna, the progenitor of all my cats, was here when we first arrived, having been left behind by the previous owner. She and the even more shabby and scraggy male who lived with her were so wild that at first it was advisable to throw food to them from a distance. But they soon learnt that the arrival of our car might mean the arrival of food. While the workmen were knocking down much of the house preparatory to rebuilding it, my wife and I were living in an hotel, and we used to carry a lot of our restaurant food away in a small plastic bag, but sometimes the bag was forgotten, and we brought nothing. The indignation and disappointment of the cats on such occasions was so hurtful that I performed the first act which convinced the villagers the English were mad —I went down to the local butcher and bought odds and ends of meat for the cats. In retrospect, I wonder how I had the nerve to do so in a country where the poorer people eat so little meat: were the Italians not so tolerant of eccentrics, they would have made my life miserable.

From that time onwards, Nonna seemed always to be an expectant or a nursing mother, and she was intelligent enough to have her kittens at the very back of the hay loft, where nobody could get at them. She would carry them down for our inspection only when they had become so large and so attractive that nobody would volunteer to drown them. Heaven knows that the heraldry experts are clever in providing impressive family trees for ambitious snobs, but they would have been very confused by Nonna. In one case, as far as I could work it out, her grandson, Grey Earl, was father of Grock, her last kitten. So Grock would appear to have been the uncle of his own father.

Thanks to the good manners she taught them, none of her

descendants asked loudly for food. She was intelligent in so many ways that I believe she knew how much more rewarding was their habit of waiting silently, with expressions of such eager confidence in the ultimate decency of man, that we were compelled, in defence of our species, to spread out a copy of *The Times* on the floor, and to drop on it pieces of our lunch. Except when there was chicken or rabbit, there was very little unseemly grabbing by one cat from another; each knew that its turn would come. Unlike most cats I have known, they ate spinach, cabbage and peas, and the rasping of their tongues on the newspaper certainly suggested that they enjoyed a vegetable diet. Even after I had folded the newspaper to indicate that they should expect nothing more, they would generally continue to sit there, gazing at me as though I were God, liable to relent. Not so, however, on days when there was chicken or rabbit or any other meat that came straight off the bone—on such occasions, Nonna always knew that she must get to the bowl outside the kitchen door to be ready for the bones off our plates. How she could tell that certain dishes would produce bones, I do not know, any more than I know how the gull which used to sit on our window-sill in Polzeath could tell which food it liked, since anything it accepted went straight down its gullet, with none of the rolling round the palate about which wine-experts talk so seriously.

When Berto left us, with Nunzia, Antonietta, his dog and all their furniture piled high on a lorry, they left their cat, Bruno—the poor beast had been so confused by the strangers who removed the chairs and tables to which he had been accustomed that when the time came for him to leave home in the lorry he could not be found. The driver was impatient to be off. Berto said he would come back on another day to fetch the cat.

He failed to do so. How could he come? He would be dependent on motor coaches—'pullmans', as they are called in Italy—and the journey from his village to ours would involve several changes and waits. Nor could I take Bruno to him in my car, for I had first to catch my cat, and he was frightened of me, and still more of Grey Earl, our tom cat of the moment. Gino would not be taking over the *contadino*'s cottage for another three months, and in the interval Bruno went wild. We were in and out of the cottage during the day. As I came in by the door, the terrified animal would jump out of the window. He would skulk in the box hedge, waiting until our own cats had had their fill of bread and odds and ends that Annunziata had put in their bowl; when the coast was clear, he would slink up to the bowl and lick it hopefully. It was summer-time, so we lunched out of doors, which meant that our own cats sat at our feet, waiting for scraps, and Bruno would watch them and us from a safe distance. If I threw some food in his direction, he would misinterpret the movement of my arm and would disappear, more convinced than ever of the injustice of human beings.

Weeks went by before we could tame Bruno enough for him to join the other cats. As soon as he had done so, he became overbearing. Only he would snatch at his food. If Grey Earl were absent, he would barge the female cats out of the way. As far as they were concerned, he was an outsider, an untouchable, a member of another and inferior caste. Often they would rather go hungry than share a bowl of milk with him. And if Grey Earl were present, he and Bruno would growl at each other until we left the table, and they were free to fight it out all over the garden. We might accept Bruno into the family circle: that was our business. But neither Nonna nor Grey Earl was going to do so.

A friend once told me that one of Colombo's notorious crows remained on his ship during the voyage from Colombo to Rangoon. It became so tame during the voyage that the passengers were as near to liking a Colombo crow as anyone could be. They were therefore distressed that, even before the ship had berthed, a squad of Rangoon crows flew out and killed it. It was much the same with Bruno—he was left alive partly because we were there to protect him and partly because he was stronger and tougher than Grey Earl. But in the end life became so difficult that, after Nonna had introduced us to another litter, carried down one by one from the hay loft, Giuseppe got out his gun and shot both Grey Earl and Bruno.

All that was a long time ago. I have lost count of the cats that have sat beneath our table since the dramatic deaths of Bruno and Grey Earl. One, The Major, deserves some paragraphs all to herself. (Yes, 'herself'. It became necessary to distinguish between two kittens, and the larger of them automatically became 'Major', despite its sex. And, after all, Bernard Shaw invented Major Barbara.) She was, in the first place, a remarkable football player, and would dribble a pingpong ball over the lawn with fantastic speed and accuracy. She was always in the court-yard, day or night, to welcome the return of the car. She would begin to purr loudly the moment I produced the newspaper at lunchtime—for her, anticipation seemed almost as good as realization. When she was very small, and still frightened to be touched, she would nevertheless begin to purr when I stroked her mother.

Professor Huizinga points out, in his *Homo Ludens*, that 'play is older than culture, for culture, however inadequately defined, always presupposes human society, and animals have not waited for man to teach them their playing'. I trained the cats so that, when I whistled for them, they would come from various parts of the garden for their walk up through the olive trees. Nonna would teach the youngest and most timid kittens to follow by uttering her distress call. We would straggle along fairly sedately until I started the game by pretending to chase one of the adult cats. They would then begin to chase each other up and down the olive trees until we reached a fork in the path, where they waited to see whether we were to go on up the hill to the three cypresses that mark the border of my land or were to turn off into the copse, where I first discovered that Major was teaching me to play.

The path is at first steep and narrow, and I have to go down it rather slowly. This would give Major the opportunity to rush ahead and hide in the undergrowth. I was expected to pretend—as I might pretend with a small child—that I could not think where she had gone. I had to pull aside the bracken or the grass, while she remained, motionless and tense, until at last I discovered her, and she raced away down the path. Once or twice, when I forgot the rules and walked on without looking for her, her disappointment was obvious; she would come along sedately at my heels, forgetting which trees she was supposed to climb—acacia trees, up which she and the others would race, paying no attention to the cruel thorns. At a certain spot, she and Grock would potter about until I had gone almost out of sight, and then, in reply to my whistle, they would come bounding along, passing me, if possible, between my legs. There was one more spot where Major would hide, and then we would all go home again.

On the evening of my seventy-fifth birthday and two years after N's death, I went for one of my walks round the small estate. The vines had come through the late frosts better than I had expected, and better than Gino had dared to hope—for even Gino, formerly so cheerful as an individual, became a pessimist when he talked about farming. '*Speriam*' *bene*'—let's hope for the best—was about as far as he would go (in which he reminded me of a Swedish friend who used to say that 'not too bad' was an Englishman's highest form of praise). The potato field was covered with small green bunches of leaves; the quince flowers near the dung heap were falling; the cherry tree was covered with small, dark blobs that had replaced the splendid blossom of a week earlier. Half of the largest field of clover had already been cut to give the cows a splendid change from their dull, dry hay.

# TUSCAN HARVEST

Under the peach trees, I found Rufus, the one remaining cat. My absences abroad had left him so timid that I seldom saw him except at meals, but he began to rub himself against a tree trunk, which is one of his ways of hinting that I should scratch his head and then stroke him vigorously down his back to his upstanding tail. I took this hint for a minute or two, and then resumed my walk up into the olive orchard.

Rufus stood in the path, watching me in a puzzled way, as though he were trying to remember something. I whistled, as I would have done in the old days. At once he remembered. For the first time in almost a year, he came running up the path after me. At the fork, he paused, as all the cats had paused in the past, to see which path I was going to take.

I took the narrow path down into the copse. At just the right moment, he came tearing down the slope, but, instead of climbing any of the acacia trees, he stopped at my feet, uncertain what to do. There was no other cat to provide companionship and competition. I left him, and walked on down the path until I was almost out of sight, and then I whistled. He should have come galloping past me, as he had always done in the past. But he sat motionless in the middle of the path. I waited for him. I called. I whistled. No use; he had finished with the world of make-believe. Ginger and white are conspicuous colours in the spring undergrowth, and for a long time I could still see a small, coloured spot in the path even when I had almost reached the house. And then I came home, feeling more lonely than I had done at any time in over two years.

## Chapter Five

'DON'T you get homesick?' compatriots ask me, holding out their glasses for a little more wine from our *cantina*. They look appreciatively towards the Pisan Hills on the far side of the valley. 'Of course, all this is very lovely, but, after all, it isn't your own country. Don't you ever feel a longing for England?'

Of course I do. A longing so keen that it becomes almost a physical pain. A longing, on any day of wind and sunshine and bright colours, for the coast of north Cornwall, with Atlantic rollers coming in majestically from a sea that is blue and green and purple, and sweeping in white foam up a wide, golden beach. A longing for the slow talk, the tankard of beer, the bread and cheese and pickled onions, in an English country pub. Of course I get homesick—how could I not be homesick for a country in which I have spent so many happy years and where I have relatives and friends?

But there are two sides to the medal. If I were living in England again, I should feel a longing that would become almost a physical pain for Tuscany. A longing, in the first place, for the sunshine and that incredible Italian sky. A longing for the little towns on hill-tops, with their civic buildings emblazoned with the arms of families that were famous centuries ago. A longing for the sense of historical continuity all around me.

Take, for example, this little city of Lucca, the towers and walls of which I see from my upstairs windows. Julius Caesar, when he was proconsul there, must have walked in the forum which I cross almost every time I go to town to do my shopping. There is a Roman amphitheatre, but not a dead and empty shell, as are most Roman amphitheatres—the oval arena is a busy fruit and vegetable market, and hundreds of people live in the patched-up galleries and boxes where the audience sat, some eighteen centuries ago. A slum? Yes, I suppose so, but there is a certain dignity about living in a slum, some of the walls of which were built by Ancient Romans. It is probable that Pope Alexander was in Lucca when he welcomed the ambassadors sent by Duke William of Normandy and declared him to be the legitimate king of England. In a Lucca church, built by San Frediano, who is better known in Northern Europe as St Finnian, lie the bones of St Richard, an English king (possibly a son of King Offa of Mercia) who died here during an eighth-century pilgrimage. William Rufus, when he came to the throne, took the oath 'by the Holy Countenance of Lucca', an ancient wooden statue of Christ which, according to legend, was carved by Nicodemus, a member of the Sanhedrin in Jerusalem who protested against the proposal to condemn him without a fair trial. Perhaps, if I were living in England, I should miss nothing about Italy as much as the warm friendliness of its people.

This is not my country? No, I suppose it isn't, although the fact seldom occurs to me. Twice a week the local farmers collect in Lucca, on the *piazza* that used to be the Roman forum, to discuss their affairs. I am not, and never shall be enough of a Tuscan to go there myself to sell a cow, but it is there that Giuseppe goes to do the job on my behalf. He wanders around until he meets a *mediatore*, a middle-man, who takes him up to some would-be purchaser. Within a few days, the purchaser and the *mediatore* drive out to the *podere*, and the bargaining begins, with Maria or Annunziata pouring out another glass of wine at each critical moment. Time after time, Giuseppe or the purchaser turns away in angry disgust, and the *mediatore* intervenes with a suggested altera-tion in the price if he senses that the disgust is becoming genuine. At last he joins their hands together, suddenly breaks the contact between them, and the deed is done, and on the Saturday following the transfer of the cow from one place to the other—the interval being necessary for the purchaser to judge whether we have told him the truth about the animal—the requisite cheque changes hands. The last of these occasions was a few months ago, when we sold our two remaining cows because they gave more work than Giuseppe and Maria can manage. That would have left us with one calf, and it was—to my amazement—Giuseppe who suggested that it would be so lonely that we might take a second calf in part payment.

I should not myself dare to undertake such a sale in the Forum, but I like to wander around there on a Wednesday or Saturday morning, for I am fascinated by the fact that I am far more conscious of being among farmers than of being among Italians—the nature of their work gives them a greater affinity with farmers in a Somersetshire market than with Italian workers in shops or factories. I am constantly

reminded of the first Italian proverb I ever learnt—*tutto il mondo è paese*, all the world's one country. If this is not my country, I seldom feel a stranger in it. In the years I have lived here, not a single Italian has made me feel I was a foreign intruder. Not one.

There are times, of course, when anger distorts my judgment—as I expect there would be if I were living in England. I get angry—as do the Italians themselves—with the bureaucrats and the absurdly conflicting laws they are expected to administer. I get angry with tradesmen who promise that some job will be done tomorrow, *'senz'altro'* (without fail), when they know that it won't be. I get angry with people who will not take their turn in a queue. I get angry with women who never deign to say 'thank you' if I hold doors open for them. Recently I got angry with two traffic policemen and, for the first time, scored over them. A rare and notable triumph.

I came on to the Florence *autostrada* at my local station, Capannori. Before leaving the entrance road, I naturally looked back to see if any vehicle was coming along the *autostrada* itself. About three hundred yards away was a small car—too far away, alas, for me to see that it was a police car. Whatever its nature, it caused me no alarm; I was so far ahead of it. I began my steady and dignified fifty miles an hour in the direction of Florence.

But within a minute this other car had passed me and signed to me to stop. *'Contravenzione,'* said the cop as soon as he reached my window. Why? I asked. Because I had failed to put out my direction arrow before I came on to the *autostrada*. But why should I have done so, since there was no other vehicle in my proximity? Because the highway code said I should have done so.

I apologized for my ignorance of that particular paragraph in the highway code, but the cop demanded a thousand *lire* and got out his little receipt book in which to record my crime. And I lost my temper. There were so many laws in

Italy that the foreigner had great difficulty in keeping up with them. Laws were brought into disrepute if they were enforced against all common sense. I had done wrong by failing to switch out my arrow, but I had put nobody to any inconvenience, let alone danger. I'd be more careful another time.

But the man took my thousand *lire*. In my own country, he said, a foreigner would have been fined for not respecting the code. He would not have been fined, I answered; he would politely have been warned. I lived in Italy because I loved Italy; I even wrote books about Italy. But my affection dwindled when an Italian policeman tried to bully me when I was conscious of having done no wrong. I became splendidly and dramatically verbose, almost as though I myself were an Italian, and finally the policeman handed me back my note. But I was carried away by my own anger and oratory. I tore the note into four pieces, and threw it away.

Before I had driven a mile, I returned to normal. The policeman, I told myself, had only been doing his job, even if he had done it without courtesy and tact. I had been a fool to lose my temper, and I had lost a thousand *lire* by doing so. But had I? It was only then that I realized I had thrown the torn note down on to the floor of my own car. I stuck the pieces together, and carefully preserved the reconstituted note until I could use it in part payment of one of my taxes.

\* \* \*

When, in 1963, I wrote *Tuscan Retreat*, the *podere* had been mine for some eighteen months. This last chapter of *Tuscan Harvest* must contain some kind of a review of my stewardship. It is not nearly as pleasant a process as I had hoped it would be when I began the first chapter.

Certainly the place is much tidier, more productive and, I think, more attractive to look at than it used to be. Gone are the pernickety little box hedges, flanking the absurdly winding paths made of white chips of marble, that made the front garden look like a miniature maze. Gone, too, are several trees, neatly standing two by two, as orderly as German soldiers, to hide the view of the Pisan Hills and the warmth of the sun. Instead, in front of the house is that rarity in Italy, a lawn, which I sow afresh each year with English lawn seed, but which is choked by weeds and coarser grasses even before the heat has had a chance to kill it. But while our new electric pump—further evidence of our efforts to be modern—can produce water from our new well, and while I am there to mow the lawn every three or four days, it still resembles a lawn. There are a few new flowers and shrubs, mostly self-sown, but they grow in a disorder as different as it could be from the carefully-planned disorder of an English garden. For more than three years a large tin of paint has taken up space in the garage, because I have been too lazy, and Giuseppe has been too busy, to paint the rusty wire fence round the pear trees. The two camellias have almost disappeared behind the ivy, whereas in the gardens of several of my friends, camellias are as common as buttercups in an English meadow. Very low marks indeed.

The farm was—perhaps still is—much more encouraging than the garden, for the people who have looked after it knew their job, whereas I did not know mine. But, again, it is much less productive than I had hoped it would be, and although the principal cause of its degeneration is Gino's illness, I know that I am largely to blame. 'Years wrinkle the skin,' I once read somewhere, 'but to give up enthusiasm wrinkles the soul.' My soul, wherever it may be and whatever it is made of, is definitely wrinkled. In the old days, even after I had virtually abandoned such activities as scything or pruning the olive trees, I still maintained at least a show of enthusiasm. I walked round the *podere* two or three times a week, and noticed enough about the progress of the crops to discuss it with Giuseppe or Gino; now my inspection takes place about once in every ten days, for Gino is no longer there to enliven the subsequent discussion with his proverbs. He is—was—the personification of the Italian definition of a peasant '*Scarpe grosse e cervello fino*'—'Heavy boots and a sharp brain.' Wherever I go in the *podere*, I see something that reminds me of his jolly, red face and his ready laughter.

But it is not fair to attribute my wrinkled soul to Gino's absence. I now seldom take the trouble to fetch the field glasses to watch some unidentified bird that has somehow escaped the men with their guns and their dogs. In any case, with whom should I now discuss its identity? Certainly not with any *contadino*, for the Italian farm-worker is amazingly ignorant of the small forms of life around him (possibly an unfair generalization, based mainly on the ignorance of Gino, Berto and Giuseppe, and on the recent assurance given me by a farmer's wife in the Chianti country between Florence and Siena. If one bird is easy to identify, both by its song and its plumage, it is the golden oriole, a bird as striking in colour as a canary and three times as large. I heard its unmistakable and melodious whistle, and she assured me it was the whistle of a blackbird. As well might one assert that a seagull was a crow.)

Given my own lessening interest, it would be excusable if the others were to lose interest as well. Gino, of course, had done so—like Berto, at the end of *Tuscan Retreat*, he had been too ill to work and, with little to do, he had sat moping in his cottage. When he came out of it, he no longer went round bare-footed and in his grey, sweat-rotted vest. Instead, he wore a jacket slung over his shoulders and a wide-brimmed hat to protect him from the forbidden sun. These, and his enlarging stomach, reminded me, most unfairly, of some drawing I must have seen in a book of my childhood of an American slave-owner in the days of Uncle Tom and his cabin. His absence from work showed in every row of vines and in every field. Giuseppe was deprived of his fifteen stone that, balancing on the harrow, had given additional bite to its prongs. Nobody now troubled to check the advance of the acacias.

Nevertheless, Giuseppe and Maria carried on with an energy that made my own laziness all the more reprehensible. The blunt truth is that I lost interest, especially since a series of doctors decided that Gino would never be able to do strenuous work again. The last of them gave him five different medicines to take each day—one in the form of a suppository, one as an injection, two as pills and one in a tablespoon—but, possibly not surprisingly, he got no better. (Italy, I believe, shares with Korea the undesirable distinction of being the only country that does not respect laws governing the manufacture and sale of patent medicines, so that any established chemist can copy any foreign medical product, give it any name he likes and sell it at any price he chooses, with the result that prescriptions mean even less to the Italian layman than they do to the layman in any other country. Thus in one year just under fifteen hundred new medicines were registered in Italy, as against just under one hundred in the United States, with four times the population.)

Gino and Maria took possession of their cottage at the far end of the pergola in May 1964 (although he had come over two or three times a week to work for us since November of the previous year). They left in October 1969, having delayed their departure so that she could help make the wine. She must be nearly sixty, but she has gone off to work in a small shoe factory belonging to one of her brothers, who has offered them both a room in his house. And Gino? He must sit there doing nothing much—since he reads only with difficulty—until he gets better. An Italian proverb claims that '*dovè entra il sole, non entra il medico*'—'where the sun enters, the doctor doesn't'—but the doctors agree that Gino must, at all costs, keep out of the sun.

I have already mentioned that Maria is one of the handsomest women I have ever seen—she retained her dignity even when she was perched on top of the rick, feeding the wheat sheaves into the threshing machine, with dark patches of sweat staining her faded blue dress. Giuseppe was a hard taskmaster, and he made no allowances for the fact that she was a woman. Nor, indeed, would she have expected him to do so—her husband was ill, and it was her duty to replace him as far as was physically possible. As with so many poorer Italian women, she seemed to gain a strength and an integrity from her religion that is lacking in most Italian men and in most women in Northern Europe or North America.

Even Annunziata, who used to spend all her time indoors, either ironing in the attic or pottering about her small kitchen, is now out at all hours of the day. The red scarf she

ties round her head takes ten years off her life, and blessedly conceals the fact that her black hair is white for the two inches nearest her scalp. Ever since N's death, I have planned to complete the translation into Italian of some of her uncompleted French recipes, and to demand of Annunziata a greater variety of diet. But I was lazy, and now it is too late— she is too busy in the fields to worry much about cooking. And I am so conscious of my good fortune in having someone who asks me every day what I want to eat that I no longer have the nerve to tell her to find some recipe in one of the cookery books we bought for her when the world was young. So when I am alone I suggest a supper of a boiled egg and some cheese, and when I have guests I take them to the restaurant down the road.

Even there, I find it impossible to respond when these guests from abroad talk enthusiastically about the excellence of Italian food. I think bitterly of the number of days in the year when I shall eat *bietola*, a plant that produces leaves like those of spinach, or veal, a meat of which no sauces can disguise the monotonous lack of flavour. The occasional visit to that little Italian restaurant, with Chianti flasks (still covered with straw, instead of with the plastic horror which has replaced it in most parts of Italy) on the tables, with people cleverly eating yard-long *spaghetti*, with views of Sicily, of Vesuvius, of St Peter's, of Venice, on the walls— that occasional visit is so pleasant a way of forgetting the fog of London or the sub-zero temperature of New York. But the food loses its attraction if one lives in Italy, with plenty of opportunity of noticing how much fat *spaghetti* adds to stomachs, bosoms and backsides.

For centuries, Italians have depended for most of their nourishment on *pastasciutta—spaghetti, maccheroni, fettucini, lasagne, canelloni* or whatever other form their excess of carbohydrates may take. *Pasta* is widely claimed as an Italian invention, but I find that Marco Polo, in the thirteenth century, took the trouble to describe the Chinese way of cutting dough into strips, and drying them in the sun, as though this were a novelty for his compatriots. In any case, it is now eaten more by Italians than by Chinese, and I wonder to what extent it may be responsible for the Italian's preoccupation with his liver—proportionately, as many Italian doctors specialize in liver complaints as American doctors specialize in psychiatry.

The prevalence of *pasta* and veal is not the fault of the Italians; it is one of the consequences of poverty, soil and climate. *Pasta* is the cheapest form of nourishment except *polenta*, made from ground maize, and until recently Italy was a very poor country. Veal is expensive, but less so than good beef would be—there is so little grazing land and what there is is so soon burnt brown by the sun, that the ordinary, small-scale farmer cannot afford to keep his calves until they grow up. I find it difficult to imagine the circumstances in which I should be sorry were I told that I should never again eat veal.

Indeed, when my wife was alive, we used sometimes to discuss quite seriously the possibility of driving all the way to Geneva, less to observe the United Nations at work than to eat our fill and over-fill of *filet de bœuf à l'estragon* in one of the city's smaller and less pretentious restaurants. Our sense of economy always overcame our sense of greed, and we consoled ourselves by assuming that the restaurant must long since have been discovered by wealthy delegates to the United Nations, that its beef probably comes now in deep freeze from the Argentine, and that the famous *estragon* sauce is probably made from a little packet bought in some supermarket. (Quite recently, I went alone to Geneva for another reason, but I found the *filet de bœuf* even better than I remembered it to have been. But possibly my enthusiasm was mainly an indication that I am a little tired of veal.)

There have been notable critics of *pastasciutta* in the past, as I learn from Elizabeth David's excellent *Italian Food\**

\* Penguin Books, Harmondsworth, 1935.

(my adjective applies rather to the book than to the food). The most notorious critic was Mussolini's loyal friend, Marinetti, the founder of Italian Futurism, who called it 'an obsolete food; it is heavy, brutalizing and gross; its nutritive qualities are deceptive; it induces scepticism, sloth and pessimism.' As if that were not enough, he added that 'a weighty and encumbered stomach cannot be favourable to physical enthusiasm towards women.' Yes, I see what he means.

\*     \*     \*

My recent visit to Geneva—apart from the *filet de bœuf*— gave me a shock; it was no longer the Geneva I knew. I had been there once during the war, at a meeting which meant the end of the League of Nations—a meeting of the League Assembly to expel one of its most important members, the Soviet Union, on account of its attack on Finland. (Germany had resigned in 1933, but German journalists who had so recently been my colleagues were there; we exchanged formal bows, but no words.) I had been there again shortly after the end of the war, at a meeting to declare that the League was defunct, but that such assets as it possessed were to be transferred to the new United Nations, with its head-quarters far away, on the other side of the Atlantic. This, we told each other, meant the decline of Geneva. I was therefore unprepared for the city's fantastic renaissance.

There were so many large and shiny new buildings, housing so many new international organizations, that it was quite difficult to identify the old Hotel National, the first home of the League. But it was in that hotel's former dining-room, overlooking a road named after that almost forgotten American, President Woodrow Wilson, that the League Council used to meet, its members sitting round a table and arguing with each other, instead of preparing speeches designed to hit the newspaper headlines. The United Nations Security Council may provide good entertainment, but it is unlikely to produce world peace—it is not merely by chance that the most successful diplomats of today are no longer those who can convey their meaning by a lift of the eyebrow or a gesture of the hand; instead, they are those who can produce the quickest and most damaging witticisms at the expense of their opponents and for the amusement of the masses.

It was in that hotel dining-room that our hopes of preventing war were all but destroyed in 1932, when the Council decided that it could do nothing to help the Chinese against the invading Japanese (with the Council blaming the absent Americans, and the absent Americans blaming the Council). At least the Americans and the Russians are no longer absent, but when President Wilson called for 'open covenants openly arrived at' he certainly did not mean that diplomatic disputes—even more difficult to settle than family ones—should be argued out in the presence of TV cameras. (In any case, there weren't any in his day.)

It was in the Salle de la Réformation, across the lake, that the French foreign minister, Aristide Briand, and the German foreign minister, Gustav Stresemann, welcomed each other on the day of Germany's admission to the League. '*Arrière les canons! Arrière les mitrailleuses!*' cried Briand in that rich, deep voice. '*Place à la conciliation et la paix!*' I was far from being the only listener who could not keep back his tears: for the first time—but for so short a time—it seemed reasonable to believe that we had, in fact, fought a war to end wars.

And it was in the former hotel bedroom upstairs that we members of the Secretariat learned to think internationally, even against what might seem temporarily to be the interests of our own countries. The League's ambitions were our ambitions. We were elated when the League stopped a small war between Bulgaria and Greece. We were in despair when Anthony Eden's efforts failed to stop Mussolini's invasion of Ethiopia. We were the young members of a young organization, hoping to fulfil an ambition almost as old as mankind.

We failed. My heroes are forgotten. Cartoons of them still hang in the Café Bavaria, where delegates and journalists used to sit, evening after evening, telling each other through the tobacco smoke how the world ought to be run, but the people who sit there nowadays pay as little attention to these portraits as to the advertisements for rival beers and *apéritifs*. Here, in Geneva, I should have felt at home. Here I had passed some of the most intense moments of my life, and now I didn't belong any more. The League's funds had been so much less than its idealism; in the United Nations, with a budget somewhere about a hundred and fifty times that of the League, the roles of finance and idealism had been reversed. I felt almost as bitter as I had felt when I came up the steps from that tiny cellar in Jerusalem, which is revered as the Holy Sepulchre, into the rival Christian churches above it, with the vulgarity of the 'sacred' relics on sale in them.

But by degrees my mood changed. The international organizations housed in all these fine new buildings were the children of the League of Nations. The few assets of the old League, some members of its staff and, above all, its objectives had been passed on to the United Nations. The old enthusiasms had gone? Well, how could it be otherwise? The officials of today could not be as innocently enthusiastic as we had been, more than four decades ago—the world had seen too much stupidity and too much brutality in the interval. They have every excuse for the cynicism which is certainly not absent from all their minds.

After all, I reminded myself, every bureaucracy has such obvious faults that we are apt to forget no government can work without one. This is an international bureaucracy, and peace without it is impossible. But these men and women of so many nationalities—so many more nationalities than in the days of the League—working side by side, year after year, must have developed some of that international loyalty that made Geneva so inspiring a city to those of us who worked there in the days of the League. Things don't come to an end with the disappearance of one individual or one organization.

And I suddenly realized one of the main reasons why I have so little to grumble about in my old age—I have believed, and I still believe, in the possibility of human progress. (And I do not, of course, mean progress in the distribution of new washing-machines or the conquest of new planets, but in the infinitely slow process of evolution.) I believe that every normal child is born with some under-standing of love and hate, of right and wrong, of justice and injustice, of kindness and cruelty—an understanding which, of course, may be developed or destroyed by the influence of its parents and its environment. I believe that it is this understanding which gives Christianity and the other great religions their power. The loneliness and suffering of Christ on his cross, for example, arouse the sympathy of other human beings and help to increase the positive side—the love, the sense of right and justice, the kindness—which is essential if the evolution of mankind is to continue. 'The older one gets,' said J. B. Priestley in an interview in the *Observer* at the time of his seventy-fifth birthday, 'the more one appreciates a certain central kindness in people.'

And yet, I believe, the value of this innate understanding is lessened, often contradicted, by the way in which every religion is taught by its priests. The more fervent their belief, the more they want to convert others to it. Because they worship God in one particular form, they want the adherence of those who worship God in another form. So many of the cruellest acts in history have been carried out by men who were profoundly 'religious'. I therefore do not believe in a 'personal' God. But I also should not wish to achieve the detachment of the Greek philosopher, Epicurus, who wrote: 'Death is nothing to us, since when we exist there is no death and when there is death we no more exist.' I cannot believe that one's awareness of beauty, justice and love is limited only to this life.

Any fool can see that the United Nations is likely to fail, as the League of Nations failed before it. The newspapers every day show that the odds against it (and us) are almost overwhelming. Evolution is a very slow process, and so many species have become extinct because they failed to adapt themselves in time to changing circumstances. *Homo sapiens* (despite the boastful name he has given himself and despite the extraordinary way in which he has gone ahead of the other animals) may become one of the failures. His progress will certainly be reversed for God knows how many centuries, unless he can learn to love his neighbours as himself (or, at least to tolerate them).

It should by now be a truism that the only realists are the idealists. One can no longer put forward as an ideal—and it has for many decades been a silly one—the conquest of one nation by another. In early days war and conquest, like slavery and superstition, had a part to play in the development of civilization; they obviously have none in these days of possible mass murder and suicide by nerve gases, hydrogen bombs and biological warfare. Obviously, unless the human race is to destroy itself or, at best, to stagnate until it comes under the domination of some other species, its members must learn to live together in peace. There can be no alternative. It is for that reason that I find more to welcome than to decry in so many of the excesses of young people today, with their contempt for the competition for the second car and the larger refrigerator and their strange sentimentality about 'love', which goes far beyond an excuse for surrender to the sexual urge.

I do not for a moment believe that we are miserable sinners. At school we used sometimes to sing a hymn, some lines of which I could never bring myself to utter—something to the effect that, even if my tears could for ever flow, all could not for sin atone. What sad and silly nonsense! And what ingratitude for the exciting experience of life! 'The man who leads a truly religious life in order to go to Heaven,' wrote Winwood Reade many years ago, 'is not more to be admired than the man who leads a regular and industrious life in order to make a fortune.' We are called upon to pray for forgiveness of our sins to an omnipotent god who made us capable of committing them. To quote further from Winwood Reade, 'pain, grief, disease and death—are these the invention of a loving God?' Why should two such honest, upright and religious people as Maria and Gino have lost so early such a loving and sweet-natured daughter as Giulietta? Why should man be a crying, cringing creature, begging for help and forgiveness?

I prefer the robust and hopeful words once written to me by that most jovial and Christian of friends, Laurence Easterbrook. 'All the great prophets,' he wrote, 'have taught exactly the same thing, namely that "the kingdom of God is within us" or, in other words, that we have the equipment to overcome every eventuality that confronts us. They also taught us the gospel of love, and assured us of the immortality of the soul. . . . If ever there were proof that something we call God does exist, it is surely that all our greatest prophets have taught much the same thing. Had their teachings been basically different, then we might indeed doubt whether there were some supreme Mind in charge of us all.'

'The kingdom of God is within us.' We know the difference between good and evil, between love and hate, between kindness and cruelty, and it is for us to make constructive use of that knowledge. We can, during this life, play our microscopic part in advancing the evolution of the human race by our support of friendship and peace between individuals and between nations, without which it cannot evolve. I can see some reason for prayer to strengthen one's courage to play that part, but not prayer for some reward in Heaven.

The reward is here and now; it gives to life a purpose and a meaning. I, for one, could wish for none better.

* * *

Alexander Pope claimed that 'the proper study of mankind is man', and the man I know best is myself.

> While scientists enlarge the scope
> Of every radar telescope
> So that, a million billion miles away they see
> Some new and splendid galaxy,
> I must admit that I am so perverse
> As still to reckon that the universe
> Revolves round me.

In this, of course, I am not alone. Each one of us is the centre of his universe. And in any case, I am now almost at the end of my self-study. The trouble about autobiography, however, is that it is so much easier to give an honest picture of somebody else than of oneself—the other fellow's defects are so much more obvious than one's own; his meannesses, his jealousies, his sulks are so much less excusable; his ambitions are so much more preposterous.

Autobiography, too, has another handicap. Bernard Berenson once quoted a young German who complained, rather engagingly, that 'everyone thinks of himself; only I think of me'.* That being so, there is the obvious risk that the reader, preoccupied by thoughts of himself, will be bored by me. I must hope that I have sufficiently aroused his sympathetic interest in Giuseppe, Annunziata, Gino and Maria to enable me to get by, as it were, in their shadow.

* *Alle denken an sich; ich nur denke an mich.*

And does one really know so much more about oneself than about other people? Recently I was shown a book written by H. R. Cummings, my old friend and boss during my years on the League of Nations Secretariat. I copied one paragraph from it, to help me to keep some sense of proportion when I become either too depressed or too pleased with myself. 'Bartlett,' the paragraph runs, 'was for a while in charge of our Information Office in London and after his resignation he, like Zilliacus, became a Member of Parliament, but not for long. He made a reputation as a broadcaster on foreign affairs. He was keenly sociable, and made many friends, but I had the impression that he was uncertain about his course. After the war, in a rather disconsolate mood I thought, he went to the Far East as a journalist, and later took up farming in Italy. I think that what he wanted most was recognition as a writer, and was a trifle overambitious, but he has published some pleasant books on his personal experiences. Maybe he is satisfied with what he has accomplished and with the reputation he has gained. There is no reason at all why he should not be.'

Dear Hal! How often Zilliacus* and I used to burst into his office in the League of Nations Secretariat in Geneva with some bright idea for furthering the hopes of peace or in some angry passion over the misdeeds of some government. And how often Hal Cummings would listen quietly, and then take his pipe out of his mouth in order to silence us with only a couple of sentences of devastating realism. Realism, not cynicism, for he fully shared our international ideals, but understood so much better than we did the lethargy of governments and the bewilderment of the governed. It was Napoleon who said that, 'to have a really free people, the governed must be virtuous and the governors must be gods', but it might just as well have been Hal Cummings.

But 'Bartlett was for a while in charge of our Information Office in London'—the 'while' was ten years of my life,

* Labour M.P., 1955-1967.

during which I convinced myself that I was worthily serving a great cause. 'A Member of Parliament, but not for long'—from 1938 to 1950, during what were probably the most critical years in the history of the House of Commons, seemed to me a very long and important stint. 'A reputation as a broadcaster on foreign affairs'—a reputation that was won by some thousands of broadcasts in various B.B.C. services, including the first broadcasts from at least a dozen foreign capitals. 'Some pleasant books on his personal experiences'—but books, nearly all passionately political, about journeys to the Communist countries in Eastern Europe or to Africa or Asia were surely a little more important than mere 'personal experiences'?

Or is his summing-up more accurate than my own, inevitably influenced by my enthusiasms, my hard work, my moments of some danger and considerable fear? Undoubtedly, he was accurate in his conclusion that I was uncertain about my course, that what I wanted most was recognition as a writer, and that I was 'a trifle over-ambitious'.

But he was wrong in concluding that I went to the Far East 'in a disconsolate mood'. I went because I had at last achieved a little wisdom; because I had realized how much my desire to reform the world was based on personal vanity— I knew as well as any dictator what was good for the masses. I once said—unjustly, as I realized when I worked for a short time during the war in his embassy in Moscow—that Sir Stafford Cripps cared too much for humanity to have time to care for human beings. That was my own danger, and my flight from Whitehall and Fleet Street was not made 'in a rather disconsolate mood', but in a spirit of mingled renunciation and adventure. Life, I had decided, was to begin at sixty.

And so, in a way, it did, for I became as never before the master of my fate and the captain of my (wrinkled) soul. I have achieved my life-long ambition after the pursuit of ephemeral success as a journalist, a broadcaster and a

Member of Parliament. As a small boy, I wanted to write books; as an old man, I sit in my Tuscan study, writing the last words of the twenty-sixth of them. How then, could I complain?

*Postscript.* The purpose of my recent visit to Geneva was not only to eat *filet de bœuf à l'estragon.* As a result of it, three weeks after I had finished this last chapter, a woman of great charm and intelligence cast doubt on her claim to the latter quality by marrying me. So life begins again at seventy-five.